El Arte de Hacer Un Cocktail y Algo Mas

•

The Art of Making a Cocktail & More

El Arte de Hacer Un Cocktail y Algo Mas

•

The Art of Making a Cocktail & More

Translated by Barbara Renard
Foreword by Anistatia Miller

MIXELLANY

English translation: © 2011 Mixellany Limited

All rights reserved. Printed in the United Kingdom. No part of this book may be used or reproduced in any manner whatsoever without written permission except in the case of brief quotations embodied in critical articles and reviews. For information address Mixellany Limited, 3 Eyford Cottages, Upper Slaughter, Cheltenham, Gloucestershire GL54 2JL United Kingdom..

Mixellany books may be purchased for educational, business, or sales promotional use.

For information, please write to Mixellany Limited, 3 Eyford Cottages, Upper Slaughter, Cheltenham, Gloucestershire GL54 2JL United Kingdom. or email jared@mixellany.com

First edition

Haredcover ISBN 13: 978-1-907434-21-1
Tradepaper ISBN 978-1-907434-22-8

British Library Cataloguing in Publication Data.
A catalogue record for this book is available from the British Library.

Contents

Foreword by Anistatia Miller 7

Appetizers 11
Cobblers 15
Cocktails 19
Collins 99
Coolers 105
Cups 109
Daisies 113
Eggnogs 117
Fizzes 121
Flips 133
Frappés 139
Highballs 143
Juleps 149
Punches 151
Hot Punches 179
Refrescos 185
Rickeys 201
Slings 205
Smash 209
Sours 213
Toddies 221
Varios 227

THE ART OF MAKING A COCKTAIL & MORE

Foreword

THE DRINKS flowed throughout Havana, in 1927, when Fernández Solana y Ca. published *El Arte de Hacer un Cocktail y Algo Mas*. Intended to be a promotional tool for La Compañia Cervecera International S.A., producers of Polar Beer and Trimalta, this volume documented 788 of the cocktails and mixed drinks that the city's bartenders were shaking and stirring for locals as well as American businessmen, journalists, and pleasure-seeking tourists who flocked to the capital's hotels, restaurants, and *bodegas*.

Over a century before Prohibition in the United States made Cuba "America's bar", Havana's *bodega* owners had been serving up icy glasses of *piña fria* (with or without rum), *ponche*, and other ingenious delights that capitalised on the cornucopia of pineapples, coconuts, key limes, lemons, and other fruits flourishing across the island. When rough *aguardiente de caña* was surpassed, in the mid-1800s, by light-bodied *ron* (Cuban-style rum), a whole new genre of mixed drinks emerged as creative *cantineros* mixed this accessible spirit with a distinctive flair for balancing fruit, spice, sweet, and sour. The Spanish love for gin and vermouth was easily translated in this Caribbean environment with some surprising twists. Some *bodegas* gave up their grocery shelves to dedicate themselves to food and beverage service. La Piña de Plata, opened in 1820, was renamed "La Florida" Don Narciso Sala Parera took ownership in 1898, catering to politicians and businessmen, who frequented the nation's capitol building situated a stone's throw away. Havana was then known as the "Little Paris of the Caribbean". The lavish beauty of its architecture, its parks and beaches, and its people lured visitors from around the globe.

American service personnel and journalists had already discovered the talents of barmen such as Emilio "Maragato" González who presided at the Hotel Plaza, around 1913, making his version of Daiquirí. They cheered, in 1910, when they sampled Rogelio's urban version of the Mojo Criollo— the Mojito—at the Hotel-Balneario's La Concha Bar.

By the time Constante Ribalaigua Vert and Miguel Boadas emigrated from Catalonia to Cuba, around 1914, La Florida was primed to become a landmark destination for American and European visitors to this tropical paradise. But it was soon joined by more casual establishments such as José Abeal y Otero's Sloppy Joe's Bar, who opened his place after returning to Havana in 1918.

Then came Prohibition and slew of new bartending blood. Eddie Woelke and Fred Kaufman arrived from New York and Britain at take their posts at the Hotel Sevilla-Biltmore. Constantino and Pete Economides arrived from New York to open the Café Sazerac. A gentlemen from Newark, New Jersey packed up his entire saloon, transported it—chairs, tables, mirrors, and bar—to a spot behind the Telégrafo Hotel, and named it after himself: Donovan's. Pat Cody opened Jigg's Uptown Bar.

The flood of globe-trotting journalists who had made their way from post-war Europe to Cuba's warmer climes relayed the message that Havana's bars were world class. In their 1927 book *Barflies and Cocktails, 300 Recipes*, Harry MacElhone and Oscar Odd McIntyre counted Sloppy Joe's amongst the world's 45 best bars on land or sea (not too shabby to be in company with Ciro's Club in London, the Taj Mahal Hotel Bar in Bombay, the Carlton Hotel Bar in St Moritz, and the Knickerbocker Bar in Monte Carlo). British playwright-journalist Basil Woon documented his love of the land and a very detailed drink-around throughout Havana in his 1928 travelogue *When It's Cocktail Time in Cuba*.

But neither of these books presented the broad scope of the *cantineros* art. In fact, despite this long tradition, only one book had ever been published on the subject before *El Arte de Hacer un Cocktail y Algo Mas*. John B Escalante's 1915 book *Manual del Cantinero* appears to be the first Cuban cocktail book. But it is the anonymously authored *El Arte* that brings to light the refinement of Cuban cocktails after a decade of emigration and cross-cultural influence had time to work their magic on the city's bar culture.

This book represents the pivotal point before La Florida and Sloppy Joe's published their famed versions of Cuban and international drink classics; before Trader Vic and Donn Beach exported more than a handful of Cuban cocktails to California, launching the Tiki craze; before Ernest Hemingway wrote the oft-repeated lines "My Mojito in La Bodeguita, My Daiquirí in El Floridita"; and before myth and legend overtook fact in the narration of so much of Cuba's cocktail history.

Of course, tastes change with time. And working with historical recipes requires a very conscious effort to adjust measurements to suit current palates and the popularity certain drink styles. But there's another lesson to be learned from reading *El Arte de Hacer un Cocktail y Algo Mas*. It is impossible to globalize food and drink, and homogenize recipes without taking into account regional and national preferences for certain flavour combinations. *El Arte* demonstrates the Cuban passion for complex yet subtle flavours accentuated a hint of sweetness as well as the *cantineros'* awareness of their audience (both local and international) and current trend. That is a lesson that none of us should ever forget. Drinks and food must appeal to the people who consume them. It's a lesson that the *cantineros* of those legendary days in the "Little Paris of the Caribbean" continue to teach us very well.

—Anistatia Miller
Mixellany Limited

BALTIMORE BRACER
1/2 Anisette
1/2 Domecq Tres Cepas Brandy
White of an egg
Shake, strain and add seltzer water.

BRAIN DUSTER
1/3 Pedro Domecq Fundador Brandy
1/3 Dubonnet
1/3 French vermouth
Shake and strain.

BRANDY CAMPRELLE
1/3 anisette
1/3 curaçao
1/3 kirschwasser
2 dashes Angostura Bitters

BRANDY CRUSTA
1/4 maraschino liqueur
3/4 Domecq Tres Cepas Brandy
A dash of lemon juice
Shake, strain and decorate with fruit

BRANDY SCAFFA
1/4 framboise syrup
1/4 maraschino liqueur
4 Chartreuse
1/4 Pedro Domecq Fundador Brandy

HUNGARIAN BRACER

1/2 Italian vermouth
1/2 American whiskey
2 dashes Angostura Bitters
2 dashes absinthe
Squeeze a lemon peel in a small glass of seltzer water and add a dash of phosphate acid.

THE ART OF MAKING A COCKTAIL & MORE

CHAMPAGNE COBBLER
Spoonful of sugar
Orange slice
Lemon peel
Fill the glass halfway with ice and add the champagne.

COBBLER ESPANOL
Orange slice
Lemon juice
Fill the glass with ice and add half champagne and half Rioja wine.

COBBLER DE VINO DE JEREZ
Fill the glass with ice
1 glass of Jerez La Ina
1/2 glass of syrup
A lemon peel
Stir and garnish with fruit.

COBBLER DE VINO PORTO
Fill the glass with ice
1/3 glass of syrup
1 1/2 glass of port wine
Stir and garnish with fruit.

COBBLER DE POLAR
Lemon juice
Pieces of pineapple
3 orange slices
Add sugar and crushed ice to the middle of the glass and fill with clear Polar Beer

COBBLER DE VINO DEL RHIN
Fill a glass with ice
1 1/2 glasses of Rhine wine
1/2 glass of syrup
2 dashes of lemon
Stir and garnish with fruit.

COBBLER DE VINO TINTO
Fill a glass with ice
1/2 glass of syrup
1 1/2 glasses of red wine.
Stir and garnish with fruit

COBBLER DE WHISKEY
Fill a glass with ice
1 glass of American whiskey
1/4 glass of Curaçao
A lemon peel
Garnish with fruit.

THE ART OF MAKING A COCKTAIL & MORE

ADAN
3/4 glass of absinthe
Dashes of orange & Angostura bitters
Shake well and serve.

ADONIS
Dashes of orange bitters
1/3 Jerez Domecq La Ina.
2/3 Italian vermouth
Shake.

ABSINTHE
A glass of absinthe
Dashes of anisette
Shake well and serve frappéed in a cocktail glass.

ALASKA
Dashes of orange bitters
1/3 yellow Chartreuse
2/3 Old Tom gin
Shake.

ALCALDE (MAYOR)
1/4 Italian vermouth
3/4 English gin
Stir well and add orange peel.

ALEXANDER
3/4 American whiskey
1/4 Bénédictine
Orange peel squeezed
Shake well.

ALFONSO XIII
1/2 pineapple juice
1/2 Cuban rum
Dashes of maraschino liqueur
Dashes of curaçao
Shake and serve in a cocktail glass.

ALMASQUE
1/3 curaçao
1/3 Jerez Domecq La Ina.
1/3 Cuban rum
Shake well.

ALMENDARES
2/3 English gin
1/3 French vermouth
Dashes of Jerez Domecq La Ina.
Dashes of curaçao
Shake well.

ALONSO NANO
2/3 triple-sec Cointreau
1/3 French cognac
Juice of 1/2 lemon
Shake and serve.

ALVARADO
1/2 Port wine
1/2 English gin
2 dashes orange bitters
White of an egg
Shake, strain and serve.

AMERICAN CLUB
1/2 American whiskey
1/2 French vermouth
Dashes of curaçao
Shake well.

ANGEL
1/4 maraschino liqueur
1/4 créme de Yvette
1/4 Bénédictine
1/4 milk

ANGEL DREAM
1/3 maraschino liqueur
1/3 crème de Yvette
1/3 milk

ANGEL KISS
2/3 Bénédictine
1/3 milk

ANTILLAS
1/3 French vermouth
1/3 Italian vermouth
1/3 Cognac Domecq Tres Cepas
Dashes of orange blossom water
Shake with crushed ice, strain and serve.

APPLEJACK
Dashes of orange bitters
1 glass of applejack
Squeeze an orange peel
Make a frappé and add an olive.

APRICOT
Juice of 1/2 lemon
3 dashes of grenadine
1/2 apricot brandy
Shake and serve.

ARDSLEY
1/2 Calisaya
1/2 sloe gin
Shake well.

ARMENTEROS
1/2 Cognac Domecq
1/2 Port wine
2 dashes Amer Picon
A cube of sugar
Shake and serve.

ARMOUR
Dashes of orange bitters
1/2 Italian vermouth
1/2 Jerez Domecq Le Ina
Shake.

ASTORIA
Dashes of orange bitters
2/3 Old Tom gin
1/3 French vermouth
Shake.

AUTOCLUB
1/2 French vermouth
1/2 Old Tom gin
1/3 American whiskey
Shake well.

AVIACION
3/4 glass of applejack
1/2 glass lemon juice
Dashes of absinthe
A teaspoon of grenadine
Shake well.

BACARDI
1/2 glass grenadine
2/3 Bacardí rum
Juice of 1/2 lemon
Shake well, strain and serve.

BALLANTINE

Dashes of absinthe
1/3 French vermouth
2/3 Jerez Domecq seco
Dashes of orange bitters

BAMBOO

1/3 Italian vermouth
2/3 Jerez seco Domecq
Dashes of orange bitters

BARACCAS

3/4 Italian vermouth
1/4 Fernet-Branca
Shake well.

BARRY

Dashes of Angostura Bitters
Dashes of crème de menthe
1/2 Italian vermouth
1/2 English gin

BEADLESTONE

1/2 Scotch whisky
1/2 French vermouth
Shake well.

BEATA
1/2 Scotch whisky
1/4 French vermouth
1/4 Italian vermouth
Shake well and serve in a whiskey glass.

BEAUTY (Linda)
1/2 English dry gin
1/4 French vermouth
1/4 Italian vermouth
White of an egg
Dashes of absinthe
A teaspoon of syrup
Shake.

BEAUTY SPOT (Lunar)
1/8 lemon juice
1/4 Italian vermouth
1/4 French vermouth
1/2 English gin
Shake well.

BIJOU
1/3 green Chartreuse
1/3 English gin
1/3 Italian vermouth
Shake.

BILTMORE
1/3 French vermouth
1/3 Italian vermouth
A little pineapple juice
1/3 English gin
Shake and serve in a tall glass.

BIRD (Pajaro)
2/3 dark curaçao
1/3 Domecq Tres Cepas
Shake well.

BISHOP POTTER
Dash of orange bitters
Dashes of Calisaya
1/4 French vermouth
1/4 Italian vermouth
1/2 English gin
Shake well.

BISHOP (Obispo)
A glass of Jamaican rum
A teaspoon of syrup
A teaspoon of red wine
Dashes of lemon
Shake well.

BLACK HAWK (HALCON NEGRO)
1/2 American whiskey
1/2 sloe gin
Shake well and a beer.

BLACK HORN
1/2 French vermouth
1/2 Old Tom gin
Dashes of curaçao
Shake in a tumbler with ice and serve in a glass.

BLANCO-HERRERA J.
1/3 French vermouth
1/3 Cuban rum
1/3 English gin
A little pineapple juice
Shake and serve.

BLANQUITA R.
1/2 Italian vermouth
1/4 French vermouth
1/2 English gin
Orange peel
Shake.

BLACKSTONE (Piedra Negra)
1/4 Italian vermouth
3/4 Old Tom gin
Shake and serve with lemon and orange peel.

BLACKSTONE EXTRA
Dashes of absinthe
1/3 French vermouth
2/3 English gin
Serve with a lemon peel

BLACK & WHITE (Blanco y Negro)
Dashes of orange bitters
1/3 Italian vermouth
2/3 sloe gin
Lemon peel

BLUE MOUNT (Monte azul)
1/2 English gin
1/2 French vermouth
2 dashes orange bitters
2 dashes crème de Yvette
Shake and serve in a cocktail glass.

BOBBIE BURNS (for two)
Teaspoon of orange juice
Teaspoon of maraschino liqueur
Dissolve a sugar cube
1/2 Scotch whisky
1/2 Italian vermouth
Shake.

BOLES
1/4 Italian vermouth
1/4 French vermouth
1/2 English gin
Orange peel
Shake with ice and serve in a glass.

BOOBY
A glass of English gin
1/3 grenadine
1/2 lemon juice
Shake well with crushed ice.

BOWMAN
1/2 orange juice
1/2 Scotch whisky
A little sugar
Mint
Shake and serve.

BRANDY (Cognac)
Dashes of orange bitters
Glass of Pedro Domecq Fundador Brandy
Dashes of syrup
Shake well.

BRANT
Dashes of Angostura Bitters
1/4 white crème de menthe
3/4 Cognac Domecq Tres Cepas
Lemon peel
Shake.

BRIDAL (Nupcial)
Dashes of orange bitters
1/3 Italian vermouth
2/3 English gin
Dashes of maraschino liqueur (Holandes)
Shake well and add orange peel.

BRIGHTON
Dashes of orange bitters
1/2 Italian vermouth
1/4 English gin
1/4 Old Tom gin
Shake well and add lemon peel.

BROOKLYN
Dashes of Amer Picon
Dashes of maraschino
1/2 French vermouth
1/2 quality American whiskey
Shake well.

BRONX

1/2 American gin
1/4 Italian vermouth
1/4 French vermouth
A slice of orange
Shake well.

BRONX DRY (Seco)

1/2 English gin
1/2 French vermouth
Teaspoon of orange juice
Shake.

BRONX TERRACE

Juice of 1/2 lemon
1/2 English gin
1/2 French vermouth
Shake.

BROWN (Carmelita)

Dashes of orange bitters
2/3 American whiskey
1/3 English gin
Shake.

BRUT (Estilo frances)

1/2 French vermouth
1/2 Calisaya
Dashes of absinthe
Shake.

BUSH (Manigua)

1/2 Italian vermouth
1/2 English gin
Teaspoon apple brandy
Shake well.

BYRRH

1/4 vermouth
1/4 American whiskey
1/2 Byrrh wine

CABINET

1/2 French vermouth
1/2 English gin
Orange peel
Stir.

CAFE DE PARIS

Glass of English gin
White of an egg
Teaspoon of milk
Teaspoon of anisette
Shake and serve in a wine glass

CAFE AU KIRSCH

Glass of kirschwasser
Glass of Domecq Tres Cepas
White of an egg
Glass of black coffee
Shake and serve in a wine glass.

CALISAYA
Glass of Calisaya
Dashes of Angostura Bitters
Shake.

CAMPUZANO PACKARD
Dashes of mint
Dashes of Angostura Bitters
1/2 Bourbon whiskey
1/2 Italian vermouth
Shake.

CAMAGUEYANO
1/2 Cuban rum
1/2 Cognac Domecq
Teaspoon of grenadine
Shake and serve.

CANDADO (Jabon)
1/2 English gin
1/2 French vermouth
2 teaspoons of raspberry syrup
Shake.

CASINO
1/2 Italian vermouth
1/2 English gin
A little créme BonBon
A little pineapple juice
4 dashes of Grenadine
Shake and serve.

CAT (Gato)
1/2 French vermouth
1/2 English gin
Shake and add an olive.

C. A. C. (Club Atletico)
1/3 Italian vermouth
1/3 French vermouth
1/3 Pedro Domecq Fundador Brandy
Orange peel
Shake.

CERVECERO
1/4 Domecq Tres Cepas
1/4 English gin
1/4 Italian vermouth
1/4 Bourbon whiskey
Shake.

CHAMPAGNE
A cube of sugar
2 dashes Angostura Bitters
A dash of Peychaud Bitters
An orange peel squeezed
1/2 Champagne

CHANTECLER
Same as the BRONX with 4 dashes of Grenadine and shake.
1/2 English gin
1/4 Italian vermouth
1/4 French vermouth
A slice of orange
4 dashes of Grenadine
Shake.

CHARLIE CHAPLIN
A little pineapple juice
1/4 French vermouth
1/4 English gin
1/4 Elixir Bacardí
A little grenadine
Shake and serve in a champagne glass.

CHERRY BLOSSOM (Flor de Cerezo)
A glass of sloe gin
A little orange juice
A teaspoon of sugar
Shake and serve.

CHINA
1/2 sloe gin
1/2 Italian vermouth
A little Domecq cognac
Shake well.

CHIQUITICA
1/3 orange juice
1/3 English gin
1/3 Italian vermouth
White of an egg
A slice of orange
Shake.

CHOCOLATE AMBROSIA
1/3 maraschino liqueur
1/3 yellow Chartreuse
1/3 apricot brandy
An egg yolk
Shake.

CINCINNATI
1/2 glass of clear Polar beer
Fill with ginger ale or soda

CLARA
1/2 Italian vermouth
1/2 sloe gin
A teaspoon of Pedro Domecq Fundador Brandy cognac
Shake well.

CLIFTON LILY
A medium size glass of ice
Dashes of lemon
2 sugar cubes
Dashes of curaçao
A glass of English gin
Garnish with mint

CLOVER CLUB
2/3 English gin
1/3 grenadine
1/2 grapefruit juice
White of an egg
A little sugar
Shake and serve.

CLOVER LEAF
Juice of 1/2 lemon
White of an egg
Glass of English gin
A teaspoon of raspberry syrup
Shake well and garnish with mint.

CLUB DE CANTINEROS
1/3 French vermouth
1/3 English gin
1/3 pineapple juice
3 dashes maraschino liqueur
Shake and serve.

COFFEE (Cafe)
1/2 teaspoon sugar
1 egg
1/2 glass Port wine
1/2 glass Pedro Domecq Fundador Brandy
Shake well and serve in a wine glass.

COLLEGE WIDOW
1/2 English gin
1/2 French vermouth
4 dashes kümmel
Shake with ice cubes and serve.

COLON
2/3 French vermouth
1/3 Angostura Bitters
Shake well.

COLONIAL O MILLER (para dos)
1/2 maraschino liqueur
Glass of Old Tom gin
Glass of grapefruit juice
Shake well and serve in a wine glass.

COMANDANTE DR. FIGUERAS
1/4 curaçao
1/4 maraschino liqueur
1/4 crème de cacao
1/4 milk
Shake and serve.

CONCHITA A.
Dash of Angostura Bitters
1/3 dark curaçao
1/3 Cuban rum
1/3 French vermouth
Shake.

CONEY
1/4 French Vermouth
2/3 Gordon gin
Stir.

CONGRESO
Glass of Domecq Tres Cepas
Glass crema de rosas
3 dashes orange blossom water
White of an egg
Shake well and serve in a wine glass.

CONSOLIDATED (Consolidado)
3/4 English gin
1/4 Italian vermouth

CORNELL
1/3 French vermouth
1/2 English gin
Stir.

CORONATION (Coronacion)
1/3 French Vermouth
1/3 English gin
1/3 Dubonnet

COUNTRY CLUB
1/2 English gin
1/2 French vermouth
Orange juice
Dashes of Chartreuse
Garnish with an orange slice and serve.

CREOLE (Criollo)
1/3 absinthe
2/3 Italian vermouth

CRESCENT
1/3 Amer Picon
1/3 Italian vermouth
1/3 American whiskey
A teaspoon of raspberry syrup
Shake, strain and serve.

CRUSELLAS R. F.
2 dashes orange bitters
1/2 English gin
1/2 French vermouth
Lemon peel
Shake.

CUBANO
Juice of 1/2 lemon
1/3 gin
1/3 Domecq Tres Cepas
1/3 Apricot brandy
Shake and serve.

CUSHMAN
1/4 French vermouth
3/4 English gin
Shake.

DAIQUIRI
3 parts Cuban rum
Juice of 1/2 lemon
Teaspoon of sugar
Shake and serve.

DAIQUIRI DULCE
1/2 Cuban rum
1/2 lemon juice
A little grenadine
Shake and serve.

DELMONICO
1/2 French vermouth
1/2 English gin
Orange peel
Shake.

DIMAS
1/2 white crème de Menthe
1/4 Pedro Domecq Fundador Brandy
1/2 crème de cacao
Shake.

DIXIE
1/2 English gin
1/4 French vermouth
1/4 Orange juice
A dash of absinthe
4 dashes grenadine
Shake and serve.

DON EMETERIO
1/2 Italian vermouth
1/4 Cuban rum
1/4 orange juice
A little grenadine
Shake and serve.

DORADO
2/3 Gordon Gin
1/3 Italian vermouth
Dashes of French vermouth
Orange peel
Shake.

DOUGLAS FAIRBANKS
1/2 apricot brandy
1/2 English gin
A little grenadine
White of an egg
Shake and serve.

DOWN (Abajo)
Dashes of orange bitters
1/3 Italian vermouth
2/3 dry gin
Shake and serve with an olive.

DREAM (Sueno)
Juice of 1/2 lemon
Teaspoon of sugar
3/4 English gin
White of an egg
Dashes of licor.
Shake and serve in a wine glass.

DUBONNET
1/2 English gin
1/2 Dubonnet
Dashes of orange bitters
Shake and serve.

DUCHESS (Duquesa)
1/3 Italian vermouth
1/3 French vermouth
1/3 absinthe
Shake well.

DUKE (Duque)
1/3 French vermouth
2/3 English gin
Shake well.

DUPLEX
2 dashes orange bitters
1/2 Italian vermouth
1/2 French vermouth
Shake.

DUTCH CHARLIE'S
2 dashes Angostura Bitters
1/3 American whiskey
1/3 Dubonnet
1/3 Italian vermouth
Shake well.

ECHARTE, J.L.
1/2 Cuban rum
1/2 orange juice
Teaspoon of chartreuse

EMERALD (Esmeralda)
Dash of orange bitters
1/2 Italian vermouth
1/2 Scotch whisky
Shake.

EMERSON
Juice of 1/2 lemon
2 dashes of maraschino liqueur
1/3 Italian vermouth
1/2 Old Tom gin
Shake.

EVA
Dash of orange bitters
1/2 Italian vermouth
1/2 Scotch whisky
Shake.

EXPRESO
Dash of orange bitters
1/2 Italian vermouth
1/2 Scotch whisky
Shake.

EWING
3 dashes Angostura Bitters
Glass of American whiskey
Shake.

FANCY (Cognac, Gin or Whiskey)
Dashes of syrup
Dashes of Curaçao
Dashes of Angostura Bitters
Glass of cognac, gin or whiskey, according to your preference
Shake and squeeze a lemon peel.

FARMER'S (Campesino)
3 dashes of Angostura Bitters
1/2 English gin
1/4 French vermouth
1/4 Italian vermouth
Shake well.

FASCISTA
10 dashes of apricot brandy
Glass of American whiskey
Dash of Angostura Bitters
Serve in glasses

FAVORITA
Lemon juice
3 or 4 sprigs of mint squeezed
Glass of English gin
1/2 bottle ginger ale
Ice in glasses and serve.

FLUSHING
1/3 Italian vermouth
2/3 Pedro Domecq Fundador Brandy
Dashes of syrup
Dashes of Angostura Bitters
Orange peel
Shake and strain into a large glass and serve.

FOUR DOLLAR (Cuatro pesos)
1/2 English gin
1/4 French vermouth
1/4 Italian vermouth

FOURTH DEGREE (Cuatro grado)
1/3 Italian vermouth
1/3 French vermouth
1/3 white absinthe
Shake well.

FOURTH REGIMENT (4.0 Regimiento)
Dashes of orange bitters
Dashes of Angostura Bitters
Dashes of celery bitters (Bitters de Apio)
1/2 American whiskey
1/2 Italian vermouth
Lemon peel
Shake.

FOX SHOT (Tiro de Zorra)
1/5 Angostura Bitters
1/5 Pedro Domecq Fundador Brandy
1/5 Italian vermouth
2/5 English gin
Shake well.

FRANCO (Aviador espanol)
1/2 cognac Domecq Tres Cepas
1/2 Jerez Domecq La Ina.
4 dashes grenadine
A little pineapple juice
Shake, strain and serve.

FRANK HILL
1/2 Cerezas Brandy
1/2 Domecq Tres Cepas
Squeeze a lemon peel
Shake well.

FRENCH CANADIAN
Dashes of absinthe
1/2 French vermouth
1/2 Scotch whisky
Shake well.

GAMBRINUS
2 dashes Angostura Bitters
1/2 Italian vermouth
1/2 sloe gin
Shake well and serve.

GIBSON
1/2 French vermouth
1/2 English gin
Shake, strain and serve.

GIN
A glass of English gin
1 or 2 dashes orange bitters
Shake well and serve.

GOLF
1/3 French vermouth
2/3 English gin
2 dashes Angostura Bitters
Shake well and strain into a cocktail glass

GOOD FELLOW (BUEN CHICO)
1/2 Italian vermouth
1/2 Bourbon whiskey
Dashes of Angostura Bitters
Dash of Calisaya
Shake well, strain and serve.

GOOD TIMES (RUMBA)
1/3 French vermouth
2/3 Old Tom gin
Lemon peel
Shake and strain into a cocktail glass.

GRAHAM
1/4 French vermouth
3/4 Italian vermouth
Shake well, strain and serve.

GRIT
1/2 Italian vermouth
1/2 Irish whiskey
Shake and strain into a cocktail glass.

GUGGENHEIM
Glass of French vermouth
2 dashes Fernet-Branca
Dash of orange bitters
Shake, strain and serve.

HABANA
1/3 Italian vermouth
1/3 French vermouth
1/3 English gin
Shake and serve with an olive.

HARRIET (ENRIQUETA)
1/2 rye whiskey
1/2 French vermouth
3 dashes of lemon
Dashes of grenadine
Shake, strain and serve.

HART
1/3 English gin
1/3 Dubonnet
1/3 Italian vermouth

HARVARD
2 dashes orange bitters
2/3 Jerez or cognac Domecq
1/3 Italian vermouth
Lemon peel
Shake well and serve.

HARVESTER
1/2 orange juice
1/2 English gin
Shake.

HEARST
Dash of Angostura Bitters
Dashes of orange bitters
1/2 English gin
1/2 Italian vermouth

HIGHSTEPPER
1/3 French vermouth
2/3 English gin
2 dashes Angostura Bitters

HILLARD
2 dashes Angostura Bitters
1/3 Italian vermouth
2/3 English gin

HIPOLITO REGUERO
1/2 Italian vermouth
1/2 Scotch whisky
Shake well.

HOLSTEIN
Dash of Amer. Picon
1/2 Cognac Domecq
1/2 Blackberry brandy

HOMESTEAD (Hogar)
1/2 Italian vermouth
2/3 English gin
A slice of orange
Serve.

HOWARD
A glass of English gin
1 or 2 dashes orange bitters
Dashes of Angostura Bitters
Shake well and serve.

HONOLULU
3 dashes of Angostura Bitters
Glass of Bourbon whiskey
Add seltzer water
Shake well.

HUDSON
1/4 Italian vermouth
3/4 English gin
A slice of orange
Serve.

HUNTER (Cazador)
2/3 American whiskey
1/3 cherry brandy
Shake well.

IDEAL
1/3 Italian vermouth
1/3 French vermouth
1/3 Gordon's gin
3 dashes maraschino liqueur
6 dashes grapefruit juice
Shake, strain and add an almond.

INFURIATOR
2/3 Pedro Domecq Fundador Brandy
1/3 anisette
Stir.

IMPERIO

1/2 English gin
1/2 Italian vermouth
4 dashes crème de cacao
White of an egg
Juice of 1/2 lemon
A little grenadine
Shake, strain and serve.

IRIS

1/2 lemon juice
2/3 English gin
Teaspoon of sugar
3 sprigs of mint

IRVING

1/2 English gin
1/4 Calisaya
1/4 French vermouth
A slice of orange
Shake.

ISABELLE

A glass of ice
1/2 grenadine
1/2 créme de cassis

ITALIANO

1/2 Italian vermouth
1/4 grenadine
1/4 Fernet-Branca

JACK ROSE
Glass of apple jack
1/2 lemon
1/4 grenadine syrup
Shake well.

JACK ZELLER
1/2 Old Tom Gin
1/2 Dubonnet
Shake.

JAPANESE
2 dashes of curaçao
1/2 Italian vermouth
1/2 American Whiskey
1/6 grenadine
Shake and serve.

JENKS
Similar to a DRY MARTINI but add a dash of Bénédictine.

JERSEY
2 dashes of syrup
Glass of apple brandy
2 dashes of Angostura Bitters

JERSEY LILY
Same as A MARTINI with a sprig of mint.

JIM LEE
2 dashes of Peychaud Bitters
2 dashes Angostura
1/2 English gin
1/4 French vermouth
1/4 Italian vermouth
Shake well.

JIMMIE LANIER
1/3 orange juice
2/3 English gin
A teaspoon of sugar
White of an egg
Shake, strain and serve.

JOCKEY CLUB
Glass of English gin
1 or 2 dashes of orange bitters
Shake well and serve.

JOSE MIGUEL
11/3 Italian vermouth
1/3 French vermouth
1/3 English gin
White of an egg
Shake well.

JUDGE (Juez)
7/8 American whiskey
1/8 Apricot Brandy
Shake.

JUVENTUD ASTURIANA
1/4 Italian vermouth
3/4 gin
Dashes of lemon
Shake and serve with a lemon peel garnish.

KISS WALTZ (Vals del Beso)
1/2 English gin
1/2 French vermouth
A teaspoon of sugar
A teaspoon of orange juice
Shake, strain and serve.

KENTUCKY COLONEL
1/4 Bénédictine
3/4 Bourbon whiskey
Lemon peel
Shake well and serve in a glass.

LADIES (señoras)
Glass of American whiskey
2 dashes of absinthe
3 dashes anisette
2 dashes of Angostura Bitters
Shake, strain and serve with a slice of pineapple.

LAVIN

1/3 pineapple juice
1/3 Cuban rum
1/3 French vermouth
White of an egg
Dashes of grenadine

LEONORA

1/4 orange juice
1/4 raspberry syrup
1/2 English gin

LEWIS

1/2 French vermouth
1/2 English gin
Shake.

LIBERAL

13 Italian vermouth
2/3 American whiskey
Dashes of Amer Picon
Shake.

LILLO

1/2 Italian vermouth
1/2 Cuban rum
2 dashes orange bitters
Shake well.

LOFTUS
1/3 Italian vermouth
1/3 French vermouth
1/3 absinthe
Shake well.

LOMA TENNIS
1/4 French vermouth
1/4 orange gin
1/2 English gin
Serve well shaken.

LONDON (Londres)
Glass of Rye whiskey
A teaspoon of syrup
2 dashes of orange blossom water
An egg
Serve well frappéed.

LONE TREE (Arbol solitario)
1/3 Italian vermouth
2/3 Old Tom gin
Stir.

LOVE (Amor)
Martini
White of an egg
Shake well.

LUCAS PEREZ
1/3 French vermouth
1/3 Cuban rum
1/3 English gin
A teaspoon of orange juice
4 dashes grenadine
Shake, strain and serve.

LUSITANIA
Dash of orange bitters
Dash of absinthe
2/3 French vermouth
1/3 Pedro Domecq Fundador Brandy
Shake well.

MANCHURIA
4 sprigs of mint with sugar
Crushed ice
Glass of Rye whiskey
Dashes of green crème de menthe
Shake, strain and serve with a sprig of mint in the glass.

MANHATTAN
Dash of Angostura Bitters
1/3 Italian vermouth
2/3 American whiskey
Shake and garnish with a cherry.

MANOLO SANTEIRO
1/3 Pedro Domecq Fundador Brandy
1/3 apricot brandy
1/3 crème de menthe
Dash of absinthe
Shake.

MARCONI
1/3 Italian vermouth
2/3 apple brandy
Shake and serve.

MARIETA
1/2 Italian vermouth
Dashes of crème de menthe
1/2 English gin
Shake and serve.

MARGOT
1/2 Old Tom gin
1/2 pineapple juice
Teaspoon of sugar
Shake, strain and serve.

MARIA M.
2/3 Italian vermouth
1/3 English gin
Teaspoon of crème de cacao
Shake, strain and serve.

MARIANAO

1/2 lemon juice
Dash of absinthe
2 Dashes grenadine
White of an egg
Glass of English gin
Shake and serve.

MARTINI

1/3 Italian vermouth
2/3 English gin
Dash of orange bitters
Stir and serve.

MARTINI (Extra)

1/3 Italian vermouth
2/3 Gordon's gin
Dash of orange bitters
Dashes of maraschino liqueur
Stir.

MARTINI DRY (Seco)

1/2 French vermouth
1/2 English gin
Stir.

MARY GARDEN

1/2 French vermouth
1/2 Dubonnet
Shake well and serve.

MARY PICKFORD
Glass of Cuban rum
Teaspoon of pineapple juice
1/2 teaspoon maraschino liqueur
1/2 teaspoon grenadine
White of an egg
Shake well and serve.

MAUSER
1/2 Italian vermouth
1/2 English gin
Teaspoon of apple brandy
Shake well.

McDONALD
Dash of orange bitters
Dash of Angostura Bitters
1/2 Gordon's gin
1/4 French vermouth
1/4 Italian vermouth
Dash of anisette
Shake well and serve.

McHENRY
1/3 Italian vermouth
2/3 Gordon's gin
Dash of orange bitters
Teaspoon of Hungarian apricot brandy
Shake well and serve.

Mc LANE
1/2 English gin
1/3 Italian vermouth
1/3 French vermouth
Orange peel
Shake well.

MERRY WIDOW (Viuda Alegre)
4 dashes maraschino liqueur
1/3 French vermouth
2/3 Italian vermouth
Shake well.

METROPOLITAN
1/2 French vermouth
1/2 Domecq Tres Cepas
2 dashes Angostura Bitters
Shake well.

METROPOLITAN (al estilo del Sur)
1/3 Italian vermouth
2/3 Domecq cognac
Dash of orange bitters
Shake and serve.

MIAMI
1/3 English gin
2/3 pineapple juice
Shake and serve.

MILLER
1/2 maraschino liqueur
Glass of Old Tom gin
Glass of grapefruit juice
Shake well and serve in a wine glass.

MILLIONAIRE (Millonario)
Dash of orange bitters
6 dashes of curaçao
3/4 American whiskey
2 dashes of grenadine
White of an egg
Shake well and serve in a wine glass.

MIRAMAR YACHT CLUB
1/3 Cuban rum
1/3 French vermouth
1/2 apricot brandy
Shake well and serve.

MILO
2 dashes Pepsina Bitters
1/3 Italian vermouth
2/3 Gordon's gin
Shake well.

MONCAYO
1/2 Cuban rum
1/2 pineapple juice
Dashes of curaçao
Shake and serve

MONTANA
1/4 French vermouth
1/2 Pedro Domecq Fundador Brandy
2 dashes of Port wine
2 dashes of Angostura Bitters
2 dashes of anisette
Shake well.

MORNING (Manana)
Dash of absinthe
Dash of Angostura Bitters
1/2 Pedro Domecq Tres Cepas Brandy
1/2 Italian vermouth
Shake well.

NANA
White of an egg
Teaspoon of sugar
Glass of Pedro Domecq Fundador Brandy
Shake well.

NARRAGANSETT
2/3 American whiskey
1/3 Italian vermouth
Dash of absinthe
Shake well and serve with an olive.

NENA A.
1/3 curaçao
2/3 Pedro Domecq Fundador Brandy
Dash of orange bitters
Shake well.

NENA R.
3 dashes Amer Picon
1/2 English gin
1/2 French vermouth
Shake well.

NEW YORK
Glass of rye whiskey
Dashes of grenadine
Dashes of maraschino liqueur
Shake, strain and serve garnished with orange peel.

NICHOLAS
1/2 sloe gin
1/2 Old Tom gin
Shake well.

NOBLE
1/2 Bourbon whiskey
3 Dashes of crème de cassis
Shake, strain and serve.

NOEL
1/2 Dubonnet
1/2 Jerez Domecq La Ina
Teaspoon of grenadine
Shake, strain and serve.

NORTH POLE (Polo Norte)
1/3 maraschino liqueur
1/3 English gin
Juice of 1/2 lemon
White of an egg
Shake well and strain into a wine glass topped with beaten milk

NUTTING
Dash of Angostura Bitters
Dash of orange bitters
1/3 French vermouth
2/3 English gin
Shake well.

OJEN
(Cocktail de Ojen a la espanola)
Glass of Ojen in a large glass with ice. Slowly add seltzer water and stir with a spoon until the glass freezes and the cocktail is made. Add a few dashes of Angostura Bitters and strain in a cocktail glass.

OLD FASHION (Estilo antiguo)
Dash of Angostura Bitters
2 Dashes of orange bitters
A piece of lump sugar
Dissolve in 2 teaspoons of water
Add a glass of the liquor you want
Serve in a cocktail glass.

OLIVETTE
3 dashes of orange bitters
3 dashes of absinthe
Dash of syrup
Dash of Angostura Bitters
1/2 English gin
1/2 French vermouth
Shake well and squeeze a lemon peel.

OPALO
1/2 French vermouth
1/2 English gin
Dash of absinthe
Shake well.

OPERA
1/2 Dubonnet
1/2 English gin
2 teaspoons crème de mandarin (tangerine)
Squeeze an orange peel
Shake well, strain and serve.

ORANGE BLOSSOM (Azahar)
1/2 orange juice
1/2 English gin
Shake well.

OSO POLAR
1/3 French vermouth
1/3 English gin
1/3 Dubonnet
Shake, strain and serve.

OYSTER BAY
1/2 white curaçao
1/3 English gin
Shake.

PALM BEACH
1/2 English gin
1/2 French vermouth
Teaspoon of sugar
Teaspoon lemon
Shake, strain and serve.

PALMA REAL
2 dashes orange bitters
1/2 Italian vermouth
1/2 Cuban rum
Shake.

PALMETTO
1/2 Cuban rum
1/2 French vermouth
Dashes of Angostura
Serve shaken.

PAN-AMERICANO
Dash of syrup
Dash of lemon juice
Glass of American whiskey
Shake.

PARADISE (Paraiso)
1/3 English gin
2/3 Apricot brandy
Shake.

PARISIAN
Juice of a lemon
Glass of Byrrh wine
Shake.

PARSON
1/3 Italian vermouth
2/3 Old Tom gin
Orange peel
Shake well.

PEBLO
Pousse café
Shake and strain.

PEACOCK (Pavo Real)
Dash of Amer Picon
Dash of absinthe
Glass of Domecq cognac
Shake.

PEPIN RIVERO
1/2 English gin
1/3 Italian vermouth
1/3 French vermouth
Orange peel
Shake.

PERLA JAPONESA
1/3 green crème de menthe
1/3 crème de cacao
1/3 Cream
Shake, strain and serve.

PERLA DE ORIENTE
1/2 apricot brandy
1/4 white crème de menthe
1/4 cream
Shake, strain and serve.

PHEASANT (Faisan)
1/2 Pedro Domecq Fundador Brandy
1/2 English gin
Stir.

PHILADELPHIA SPECIAL
1/3 Italian vermouth
2/3 English gin
Dashes of curaçao
Shake, strain and serve.

PICK ME UP (LEVANTAME)
1/3 Pedro Domecq Tres Cepas Brandy
1/3 Italian vermouth
1/3 absinthe
Shake well.

PICON
1/4 Italian vermouth
3/4 Amer Picon
Orange peel
Stir.

PINE TREE (PINO)
1/3 Ferrero vermouth
2/3 Gordon's gin
Mint
Shake.

PING-PONG
1/2 sloe gin
1/2 crème de Yvette
3 dashes of lemon juice
Shake well.

PIÑA BLOSSOM

1/4 Italian vermouth
1/4 French vermouth
1/4 English gin
1/4 pineapple juice
Shake, strain and serve.

PIÑA BRONX

1/2 pineapple juice
1/2 Cuban rum
3 dashes of curaçao
Shake, strain and serve.

PLAYA MARIANAO

1/3 lemon juice
1/3 English gin
1/3 apricot brandy
5 dashes grenadine
Shake well.

PLAZA HOTEL

1/4 Italian vermouth
3/4 English gin
A slice of pineapple
Shake.

PLUS ULTRA ESPANOL

1/2 sloe gin
1/2 French vermouth
Dashes of orange
Teaspoon of sugar
Shake, strain and serve.

POEMA
1/3 French vermouth
2/3 English gin
Dashes or orange bitters
Dashes of Bénédictine
Shake.

POLAR
1/2 Domecq cognac
1/2 Jerez Oloroso (scented)
3 dashes of grenadine
Shake, strain and serve with an almond.

POLO FARM
1/3 French vermouth
2/3 English gin
Rinse a cocktail glass with cognac.

POLO
1/3 grapefruit juice
1/3 orange juice
1/3 Old Tom gin
Shake and serve in a wine glass.

PORTER OR PAT'S
1/2 English gin
1/4 French vermouth
6 dashes of Italian vermouth
Dashes of curaçao
Lemon peel.
Sprig of mint
Shake.

PRAIRIE (Pradera)

A glass of Old Tom gin
An egg, salt and pimiento

PRESIDENTE

1/2 Cuban rum
1/2 French vermouth
Dashes of grenadine
Stir, strain and serve garnished with orange peel.

PRESIDENTE MACHADO

1/2 Cuban rum
1/2 French vermouth
Dashes of grenadine
Dashes of curaçao
Stir.

PRIMO DE RIVERA

1/2 Italian vermouth
1/2 cognac
A little pineapple juice
A teaspoon of sugar
3 dashes of lemon
Shake, strain and serve.

PRINCESS LILLIAN

1/2 English gin
1/2 French vermouth
1/2 teaspoon of white crème de menthe
1/2 teaspoon crème de Yvette.
Shake, strain and serve.

PRINCIPE DE ASTURIAS
(Prince of Asturias)
1/3 white crème de menthe
1/3 English gin
1/3 Italian vermouth
Shake.

PRINCIPE DE GALES (Prince of Wales)
Dash of orange bitters
1/3 Italian vermouth
1/3 Gordon's gin
1/3 white crème de menthe
Serve well shaken.

PRINCETON
Glass of English gin
1 or 2 dashes of orange bitters
Splash of carbonated mineral water
Shake well and serve.

PUENTES
1/2 French vermouth
1/2 English gin
Teaspoon of Chartreuse
Orange peel
Shake.

QUEEN (Reina)

1/2 English gin
1/2 French vermouth
Teaspoon of pineapple juice
Teaspoon of sugar
Shake, strain and serve.

REIS

2 dashes of Angostura Bitters
2 dashes of absinthe
Glass of English gin
Shake.

RIDING CLUB
(Club de Equitacion)

Glass of Calisaya
Dash of Angostura Bitters
3 dashes of phosphate acid
Shake.

ROB ROY

1/2 Italian vermouth
1/2 Scotch whisky
Dash of Angostura Bitters
Dash of orange bitters

ROBERT BURNS

Dashes of absinthe
1/4 Italian vermouth
3/4 Scotch whisky
Shake well.

ROMANO
3 dashes of Calisaya
Glass of Scotch whisky
Shake well and serve with a cherry.

ROSA
1/5 orange juice
1/5 grenadine syrup
1/2 English gin
Shake well.

ROSSINGTON
1/3 Italian vermouth
2/3 Old Tom gin
Orange peel
Shake well.

ROYAL SMILE (Sonrisa Real)
Juice of half an orange
1/2 glass of grenadine
1/2 glass of French vermouth
1/2 glass of apple brandy
White of an egg
Shake and serve in a wine glass.

RUBIN
1/2 English gin
1/2 French vermouth
Dashes of pineapple juice
Dashes of crème Bon-Bon
Shake, strain and serve.

RUBY
Dash of Grenadine
Teaspoon of apple jack
3/4 English gin
Shake well.

RUBY ROYAL
1/2 sloe gin
1/2 French vermouth
2 dashes of raspberry liqueur
Shake well and add a cherry.

SABBATH (Sabatino)
1/3 Pedro Domecq Fundador Brandy
1/3 Port wine
An egg
1/3 coffee (cafe)
1/2 teaspoon of sugar
Shake and strain into a wine glass.

SALOME
1/4 Italian vermouth
1/4 French vermouth
1/4 Cuban rum
2 dashes of orange bitters
Shake with 3 celery leaves.

SANSON

1/2 Cuban rum
1/2 Italian vermouth
Dashes of curaçao
Dashes of grenadine
Shake, strain and serve with an orange peel.

SARATOGA

2 dashes of pineapple juice
2 dashes of maraschino liqueur
Dash of orange bitters
Glass of Domecq cognac

SARDINERO

Teaspoon of Curaçao
1/2 Italian vermouth
1/2 apple jack
Dash of orange bitters
Shake, strain and serve.

SAXON

Glass of Cuban rum
Juice of 1/2 lemon
2 dashes of grenadine

SCHEUER

1/2 Dubonnet
1/2 Italian vermouth
Shake and add a dash of Angostura.

SEÑORITA
3/4 maraschino liqueur
1/4 milk

SEPTEMBER MORNING
(Manana de Stbre.)
Dashes of lemon
1/2 French vermouth
1/2 English gin
3 dashes of Apricotine
Shake, strain and serve.

SERGIO CARBO
White of an egg
1/3 Cuban rum
13 Italian vermouth
1/3 orange juice
Teaspoon of grenadine
Shake and serve.

SHERMAN
1/3 Italian vermouth
2/3 American whiskey
Dash of absinthe
Shake.

SHERRY (Jerez)
Glass of Jerez Domecq La Ina.
Dash of orange bitters
Dash of Angostura Bitters

SILVER (Plata)
2 dashes orange bitters
1/3 Italian vermouth
2/3 English gin
2 dashes of maraschino liqueur
Shake.

SLOME
1/3 Bourbon whiskey
1/3 Pedro Domecq Fundador Brandy
1/3 Dubonnet
Shake well.

SLOPPY JOE
1/3 pineapple juice
1/3 Pedro Domecq Fundador Brandy
1/3 Port wine
Dashes of grenadine and curaçao

SMITH
1/2 Pedro Domecq Fundador Brandy
1/2 apricot brandy
Teaspoon of crème de menthe
Shake and add a dash of absinthe.

SOCIETY (Sociedad)
1/3 English gin
2/3 French vermouth
Dash of grenadine
Shake.

SODA
3 dashes of Angostura Bitters
Lemon peel
1/2 bottle lemon soda
A piece of ice
Teaspoon of sugar
Serve in a large glass.

SOUL KISS (Beso del alma)
1/3 American whiskey
1/3 Dubonnet
1/3 French vermouth
Teaspoon of orange juice
Shake.

SOUTH AFRICA (Africa del Sur)
1/2 Jerez Domecq La Ina
Dash of Angostura Bitters
1/2 English gin
3 dashes of lemon juice

SOUVENIR
1/2 French vermouth
1/2 English gin
4 dashes of crème de noyaux
Shake, strain and serve.

SPAULDING
1/3 Dubonnet
2/3 English gin
Teaspoon of Scotch whisky
Shake well.

SPHINX (Esfinge)
2/3 English gin
1/6 Italian vermouth
1/6 French vermouth
Thin lemon peel
Shake.

ST. FRANCIS (San Francisco)
1/2 French vermouth
1/2 English gin
Dashes of Angostura Bitters

ST. JOHN (San Juan)
1/3 Italian vermouth
2/3 Old Tom gin
Dash of orange bitters
Stir, strain and serve.

ST. PETER (San Pedro)
Glass of English gin
Dashes of lemon
Dashes of syrup
Shake.

STAR (Estrella)
Dash of orange bitters
1/2 apple jack
1/2 Italian vermouth
Shake with a lemon peel.

STAR (A LA ANTIGUA)
Teaspoon of sugar
Dash of orange bitters
2/3 apple jack
1/2 Italian vermouth
Slice of orange and a sprig of mint.

STEINHART
1/3 French vermouth
1/3 Fundador cognac
1/3 white crème de menthe
Shake, strain and serve.

STORY (CUENTO)
1/2 Angostura Bitters
1/4 strawberry juice or juice of 3 strawberries
Dash of maraschino liqueur
Glass of Domecq cognac
Shake.

SUNSHINE (LUZ SOLAR) FOR TWO
Lemon juice
1/2 French vermouth
1 1/2 Old Tom gin
Teaspoon of grenadine
White of an egg for each
Shake and serve in a wine glass.

SUNSET (Puesta de Sol)
1/2 Italian vermouth
1/2 English gin
Teaspoon of grenadine
Teaspoon of orange juice
Shake, strain and serve.

SWAN (Cisne)
3 dashes of lemon juice
2 dashes of Angostura Bitters
1/2 French vermouth
1/2 English gin
Shake.

TAXI
1/2 French vermouth
1/2 English gin
2 teaspoons of lemon juice
2 teaspoons of absinthe
Serve well shaken.

TANGO
1/3 Italian vermouth
2/3 English gin
1/2 teaspoon apricot brandy
Shake well, strain and serve.

TIQUI
1/3 Italian vermouth
1/3 Cuban rum
1/3 maraschino liqueur
Add pineapple juice.

TIP TOP
Glass of French vermouth
4 dashes of Bénédictine
Dash of Angostura Bitters
3 dashes of orange bitters
Shake.

TITINA
1/2 Cuban rum
1/2 pineapple juice
3 dashes of Angostura Bitters
3 dashes of maraschino liqueur
Shake, strain and serve.

TORONJA BRONX
1/4 Italian vermouth
1/4 French vermouth
1/4 English gin
1/4 grapefruit juice
Shake, strain and serve.

TREASURY (Tesoreria)
1/3 Italian vermouth
2/3 Gordon's gin
Slice of orange
Serve well shaken.

TRILBY
Dash of orange bitters
2/3 Old Tom gin
1/6 French vermouth
1/6 crème de Yvette
Shake well and add a cherry.

TRINIDAD
1/2 English gin
4 dashes of maraschino liqueur
Shake, strain and serve with a celery stock.

TROWBRIDGE
Dash of orange bitters
2/3 French vermouth
1/3 English gin
Orange peel.

TRUFFIN
1/3 Dubonnet
1/3 Domecq Tres Cepas cognac
1/3 absinthe
Shake, strain and serve.

TULANE
1/2 Italian vermouth
1/2 English gin
1/2 teaspoon strawberry brandy
Shake with a little ice, strain and serve.

TURF ARGENTINO

2 dashes orange bitters
2 dashes maraschino liqueur
1 drop absinthe
1/2 French vermouth
1/2 English gin

TURF AMERICANO

2 dashes Angostura Bitters
1/3 Italian vermouth
2/3 Dutch gin
Shake.

TU Y YO

1/3 Jerez Domecq La Ina.
2/3 English gin
2 dashes orange bitters
Shake.

TUXEDO

Dash of maraschino liqueur
3 dashes of Angostura Bitters
Dash of absinthe
2/3 English gin
1/3 French vermouth
Teaspoon of Jerez Domecq La Ina.
Shake well.

TWO SPOT (Dos maracas)
1/2 Pedro Domecq Fundador Brandy
1/2 dark curaçao
Shake and strain in a cocktail glass. Squeeze a lemon peel.

ULLOA
1/2 pineapple juice
1/2 Cuban rum
2 dashes maraschino liqueur
2 dashes of Curaçao
Shake, strain and serve.

UNION CLUB (Habana)
1/2 French vermouth
1/2 Gordon's gin
Dash of absinthe.

UNION CLUB
Dash of orange bitters
1/3 Port wine
2/3 gin
Shake well.

UZCUDUM
1/2 Trimalta
1/2 clear Polar Beer
Yolk of an egg
Shake well.

VALENTINO
2/3 gin
1/3 Italian vermouth
Dashes of crème de menthe.

VAN WYCK
1/2 Sloe Gin
1/2 English gin
2 dashes of orange bitters.
Shake well.

VEDADO TENNIS
Dash of apricot brandy
1/2 French vermouth
1/2 English gin
Shake.

VERMOUTH ACHAMPANADO
In a medium glass with crushed ice, put a teaspoon of sugar, pour Italian vermouth half way and add soda for the rest.

VERMOUTH LA AMERICANA
Glass of Italian vermouth
2 dashes of Angostura Bitters
1/2 teaspoon sugar
Adorn with a cherry.

VERRACO
1/4 Cuban rum
1/4 brandy
1/4 Cognac Domecq
1/4 gin
Dashes of bitters

VETERANO
Glass of Cuban rum
Glass of yellow Chartreuse
4 dashes of grenadine
4 dashes of absinthe
Shake, strain and serve.

VIENNA
1/2 Italian vermouth
1/2 French vermouth
Dash of absinthe
Serve frapéed.

VIRGEN LOCA
1/2 Gordon's gin
1/2 Italian vermouth
2 dashes of raspberry syrup
2 dashes of Angostura Bitters
Shake.

VOLUNTARIO

Glass of Italian vermouth
3 dashes of Angostura Bitters
3 dashes of Amer Picon.
Teaspoon of sugar
Crushed ice. Strain using a barspoon.

WALDORF

1/3 American whiskey
1/3 Italian vermouth
1/3 absinthe
2 dashes orange bitters
Shake.

WALDORF SPECIAL

Juice of one lemon
Glass of Apricotine
Shake well and serve in a cocktail glass.

WALDORF QUEEN'S

2 pieces of pineapple
1/2 English gin
1/4 French vermouth
1/4 Italian vermouth
Small slice of orange
Shake well, strain and serve in a cocktail glass.

WARD LINE
1/4 English gin
1/4 green crème de menthe
1/4 kümmel
1/4 fresh milk
Teaspoon of sugar

WAXEN
1/4 Italian vermouth
1/4 apple brandy
1/4 yellow Chartreuse
1/4 Old Tom gin

WEST INDIA (Antilla)
2 dashes of Angostura Bitters
1/2 French vermouth
2 lemon peels
Shake.

WHILE AWAY (Ausente)
1/3 white crème de menthe
2/3 Wolfe gin

WHISKEY
2 dashes of Angostura Bitters
A lump of sugar
Glass of Bourbon whiskey
Lemon peel.

WHITE ELEPHANT (Elefante blanco)
1/3 Italian vermouth
2/3 English gin
White of an egg.
Shake well.

WHITE RAT (Rata blanca)
3/4 absinthe
1/4 anisette
Shake well.

WHITE ROSE (Rosa blanca)
1 glass aromatic gin
1/2 glass de maraschino liqueur
Juice of 1/4 orange
Juice of a lemon
White of an egg.

WILSON
1/2 English gin
1/2 French vermouth
2 dashes of absinthe
Shake, strain and serve with a small onion.

WILLIAM GODRON
Teaspoon of sugar
Juice of 1/2 lemon
3 dashes of Angostura Bitters
3 dashes of raspberry syrup
Glass of Cuban rum
Shake well.

WONDER (Milagro)
1/3 Italian vermouth
2/3 English gin
Piece of pineapple
Shake well.

YACHT CLUB
1/3 sloe gin
1/3 Italian vermouth
1/3 juice of orange or grapefruit
4 dashes crème de cacao
4 dashes of grenadine
Shake, strain and serve.

YALE
Dash of orange bitters
Dash of absinthe
Glass of Old Tom gin
Lemon peel
Shake.

YANKEE
Teaspoon of orange juice
1/4 Grand Marnier
3/4 English gin
1 filbert nut
Shake well.

YANKEE PRINCESS (Princesa Yankee)
2/3 English gin
1/3 Grand Marnier
Shake and serve with a cinnamon stick.

YORK
2 dashes of orange bitters
1/2 French vermouth
1/2 Scotch whisky
Serve well frappéed.

ZABRISKIE
Dash of orange bitters
Dash of maraschino liqueur
Dash of Angostura Bitters
2/3 English gin
1/3 Italian vermouth
Shake well.

ZAZARAC
1/2 lump of sugar
Dash of Angostura Bitters
Dash of orange bitters
Dash of anisette
Glass of American whiskey
Squeeze a lemon peel
Add three dashes of absinthe and serve in a tall glass.

ZAZA
1/2 English gin
1/2 Dubonnet
Dash of Angostura Bitters

ZORRICHIQUI
1/3 orange Juice
1/3 Italian vermouth
1/3 jerez Oloroso de Domecq
Dashes of Chartreuse

ZORRILLA
1/2 Italian vermouth
1/2 jerez Oloroso de Domecq
Dashes of Cuban rum elixir
Dash of curaçao
Shake and serve.

THE ART OF MAKING A COCKTAIL & MORE

BOURBON COLLINS

Glass with ice
Juice of a small lemon
Teaspoon of sugar
Glass of Bourbon whiskey
Stir. Strain into a large glass and add a bottle of soda. Stir with a spoon.

BRANDY COLLINS

Glass with ice
Juice of a small lemon
Teaspoon of sugar
Glass of Pedro Domecq Fundador Brandy cognac.
Stir. Strain into a large glass and add a bottle of soda. Stir with a spoon.

IRISH COLLINS

Glass with ice
Juice of a small lemon
Teaspoon of sugar
Glass of Irish whiskey
Stir. Strain into a large glass and add a bottle of soda. Stir with a spoon.

JOHN COLLINS
Glass with ice.
Juice of a small lemon
Teaspoon of sugar
Glass of Dutch gin.
Stir. Strain into a large glass and add a bottle of soda. Stir with a spoon.

RUM COLLINS
Glass with ice
Juice of a small lemon
Teaspoon of sugar
Glass of Cuban rum
Stir. Strain into a large glass and add a bottle of soda. Stir with a spoon.

RYE COLLINS
Glass with ice
Juice of a small lemon
Teaspoon of sugar
Glass of Rye whiskey
Stir. Strain into a large glass and add a bottle of soda. Stir with a spoon.

SCOTCH COLLINS
Glass with ice
Juice of a small lemon
Teaspoon of sugar
Glass of Scotch whisky
Stir. Strain into a large glass and add a bottle of soda. Stir with a spoon.

TOM COLLINS
Glass with ice
Juice of a small lemon
Teaspoon of sugar
Glass of English gin
Stir. Strain into a large glass and add a bottle of soda. Stir with a spoon.

THE ART OF MAKING A COCKTAIL & MORE

EDITOR'S NOTE:
None were listed in this book.
There was only a blank page.

THE ART OF MAKING A COCKTAIL & MORE

THE ART OF MAKING A COCKTAIL & MORE

EDITOR'S NOTE:
None were listed in this book.
There was only a blank page.

THE ART OF MAKING A COCKTAIL & MORE

BRANDY (De cognac)
Juice of 1/2 lemon
1/2 glass of raspberry syrup
Glass of Perdro Domecq Tres Cepas Brandy
In a thin glass with fruit.

CHOCOLATE
Juice of a lemon
1/2 glass of Domecq Tres Cepas
1/2 glass of Port wine
1/3 glass of raspberry syrup
Glass with chipped ice and fruit.

GIN (De ginebra)
Juice of 1/2 lemon
Glass of English gin
1/2 glass of raspberry syrup
In a glass with chipped ice and fruit.

GINGER (de Jenjibre)
Juice of 1/2 lemon
1/2 teaspoon of sugar
1/2 glass of English gin
1/2 glass of Pedro Domecq Fundador Brandy
Shake with chipped ice and serve in a glass with fruit and peppermint.

HIGHLAND (Montana)
Juice of 1/2 lemon
Juice of 1/2 orange
2/3 glass of Scotch whisky
Glass of syrup
Serve in glass with fruit and peppermint.

JUNE (Junio)
Juice of 1/2 lemon
Juice of 1/2 orange
1/2 glass of raspberry syrup
Add Ginger Ale and adorn with fruit.
Serve in a glass with chipped ice.

RON
Juice of 1/2 lemon
Glass of Cuban rum
1/2 glass of raspberry syrup
In a glass with chipped ice and adorn with fruit.

STAR (Estrella)
Juice of 1/2l lemon
1/2 glass of English gin
1/2 glass of Apple Jack
1/2 glass of Grenadine
In a glass with chipped ice and adorned with fruit.

WHISKEY
Juice of 1/2 lemon
Glass of Scotch whisky
1/2 glass of raspberry syrup
In a glass with chipped ice and fruit.

COGNAC (BRANDY)

1 egg
Glass of Pedro Domecq Fundador Brandy
Dashes of Cuban rum
Teaspoon of sugar
Milk
Shake, strain and a sprinkle of nutmeg.

JEREZ (SHERRY)

3 parts Jerez Domecq
1 egg yolk
Sugar
Shake in a cocktail shaker. Serve in a medium glass and garnish with powdered cinnamon.

JEREZ CON HUEVO

Teaspoon of Jerez Domecq La Ina.
An egg
Fill a glass with Sherry wine until the egg floats.

RON

Glass of Cuban rum
Teaspoon of sugar
1 egg
Milk
Shake, strain and add grated nutmeg.

VERMOUTH

3 parts vermouth

1 egg yolk

Sugar

Shake (en cotelera), serve in a medium glass with powdered cinnamon.

WHISKEY

Glass of Bourbon whiskey

Dashes of Cuban rum

1 egg

Teaspoon of sugar

Milk

Shake, strain and sprinkle nutmeg.

Fizzes Achampañados

AMER PICON POUFFLE

Glass of Amer Picon
Glass of Grenadine
White of an egg
Shake, strain and fill the rest of the glass with seltzer water

ANGOSTURA

Juice of 1/2 lemon
Teaspoon of sugar
1/2 glass of Angostura Bitters
White of an egg
Teaspoon of cream
Shake well, strain and fill the glass with seltzer water.

BAYARD

Juice of 1 1/2 lemons
Teaspoon of sugar
Glass of English gin
Dashes of maraschino liqueur
Dash of raspberry syrup
Shake, strain and and fill glass with syphon water.

BIRD OF PARADISE (AVE DEL PARAISO)

1/2 lemon
Teaspoon of sugar
Glass of English gin
White of an egg
Dash of raspberry syrup
Shake, strain into a large glass and fill with seltzer water.

BISMARCK
Juice of 1/2 lemon
Teaspoon of sugar
1 egg
Glass of Sloe Gin
Fill glass with seltzer and shake.

BRANDY (DE COGNAC)
Juice of 1 lemon
Teaspoon of sugar
Glass of Pedro Domecq Fundador Brandy
Shake, strain into a glass with seltzer water. Add 3 dashes of yellow Chartreuse.

CANADIAN (CANADIENSE)
Juice of 1 lemon
Teaspoon of sugar
Glass of English gin
1 egg
Shake, strain and fill glass with seltzer.

CANADIAN WHISKEY (DE WHISKEY CANADIENSE)
Juice of 1/2 lemon
Teaspoon of sugar
Glass of Canadian whiskey
Shake, strain and fill glass with seltzer.

CHICAGO
Juice of 1/2 lemon
Teaspoon of sugar
1/2 glass of Cuban rum
1/2 glass of Port wine
White of an egg
Shake, strain and fill glass with seltzer.

CLARET (DE VINO TINTO)
Juice of 1/2 lemon
1/2 glass of orange juice
2/3 glass of Domecq Tres Cepas
Shake, strain and fill glass with seltzer.

DAISY
Juice of 1/2 lemon
1/2 glass of orange juice
2/3 glass of Domecq Tres Cepas
Shake, strain and fill glass with seltzer.

DIAMOND (DIAMANTE)
Juice of 1/2 lemon
Teaspoon of sugar
Glass of English gin
Shake, strain and fill glass with champagne.

DRY GIN FIZZ
Juice of 1/2 lemon
Teaspoon of sugar
Glass of dry English gin
Shake, strain and fill glass with seltzer.

GALVEZ
Juice of 1 lemon
Teaspoon of sugar
4 dashes of raspberry syrup
Glass of English gin
White of an egg
Dash of orange blossom water
Glass of cream
Shake well, strain into a large glass and fill with seltzer.

GIN (de Ginebra)
Juice of 1/2 lemon
Teaspoon of sugar
Glass of English gin
Shake, strain and fill glass with seltzer.

GLORIA SWANSON
1/2 lemon, chopped
2 crushed strawberries
Glass of English gin
White of an egg
Dash of orange blossom water
Glass of cream
Shake, strain into a large glass and fill with seltzer.

GOLDEN (de Oro)
Juice of 1/2 lemon
Teaspoon of sugar
Glass of English gin
A yolk of an egg
Shake, strain and fill glass with seltzer.

GRAND DUKE
Glass of English gin
4 dashes of maraschino liqueur
4 dashes of orange juice
A little cream
Shake and serve in a medium glass.

GRENADINE (Granadina)
Juice of 1/2 lemon
1/2 glass of grenadine syrup
Glass of Old Tom gin
Shake, strain and fill glass with seltzer.

HOLLAND (Holanda)
Juice of 1/2 lemon
Teaspoon of sugar
Glass of Holland gin
Dash of white crème de menthe
Shake, strain and fill glass with seltzer.

IRISH (Irlandes)
Juice of 1/2 lemon
Teaspoon of sugar
Glass of Irish whiskey
Shake, strain into a large glass and fill with seltzer water.

JAP (Japones)
Juice of 1/2 lemon
Teaspoon of sugar
White of an egg
1/2 glass of Port wine
1/2 glass id Rye whiskey
Shake, strain into a large glass and fill with seltzer water.

KING COLE
Gin Fizz with grenadine syrup
Frappé well.

LALLA HOOK
Juice of 1/2 lemon
Teaspoon of sugar
1/3 glass of Vanilla
1/3 glass of Pedro Domecq Fundador Brandy cognac
1/3 glass of Cuban rum
A teaspoon of cream
Shake, strain and fill glass with seltzer water.

MERRY WIDOW (Viuda Alegre)
Juice of 1/2 lemon
Juice of 1/2 orange
Teaspoon of sugar
Glass of English gin
White of an egg
Shake well, strain into a large glass and fill with seltzer water.

MEXICO
Juice of 1/2 lemon
Juice of 1/2 orange
1/2 glass of Grenadine
Glass of Rhine wine
Shake, strain and fill glass with seltzer.

MORNING GLORY
Juice of 1/2 lemon
2 dashes of absinthe
White of an egg
Glass of Scotch whisky
Teaspoon of sugar
Shake, strain and fill glass with seltzer.

NEW ORLEANS
(Nueva Orleans)
Juice of 1/2 lemon
2 dashes of orange blossom water
Teaspoon of sugar
Glass of cream
Glass of English gin
White of an egg
Shake, strain into a large glass and fill with seltzer water.

POLLY
Gin Fizz made with grenadine in place of sugar.

REMUS

Juice of 1/2 lemon
Dash of grenadine
Dash of lemon juice
Teaspoon of sugar
Glass of English gin
1/2 glass of cream

Shake well, strain into a large glass and fill with seltzer water.

ROYAL GIN (Ginebra Real)

Juice of 1/2 lemon
Teaspoon of sugar
Glass of English gin
White of an egg

Shake, strain and fill glass with seltzer.

SCOTCH WHISKY (de whiskey Escoces)

Juice of a small lemon
Teaspoon of sugar
Glass of Scotch whisky

Shake, strain and fill glass with seltzer.

SILVER (Plata)

Juice of 1/2 lemon
Teaspoon of sugar
Glass of English gin
White of an egg

Shake, strain into a large glass and fill with seltzer water.

SILVER BOWL
SNOW BOWL
(Taza de plata o nevada)
Glass of grapefruit juice
1/2 glass of English gin
1/2 glass of Rhine wine
2 dashes of orange blossom water
Shake well and strain.

SLOE GIN FIZZ
Juice of 1/2 lemon
Teaspoon of sugar
Glass of sloe gin
Shake, strain and fill glass with seltzer.

SUNSHINE (Luz Solar)
Juice of 1/2 lemon
Juice of 1/2 orange
White of an egg
Glass of Irish whiskey
Shake, strain into a large glass and fill with seltzer water.

STRAWBERRY (de Fresa)
Juice of 1/2 lemon
1/4 teaspoon of sugar
6 strawberries
Glass of Old Tom gin
Shake, strain and fill with seltzer water.

TOM GIN FIZZ
Juice of 1/2 lemon
Teaspoon of sugar
Glass of Old Tom Gin
Shake, strain and fill glass with seltzer.

VIOLET (Violeta)
Juice of 1/2 lemon
Teaspoon of sugar
3/4 glass of English gin
1/4 glass of crème de violette
Shake, strain into a fizz glass and fill with seltzer water.

WALDORF
Juice of an orange
Juice of a lemon
1 egg
Teaspoon of sugar
Shake, strain and fill glass with seltzer.

WHISKEY
Juice of 1/2 lemon
Teaspoon of sugar
Glass of Bourbon or Rye, whichever you prefer
Shake, strain and fill glass with seltzer water.

WHISKEY-GRANADINA
Juice of 1/2 lemon
1/3 glass of grenadine
2/3 glass of Bourbon or Rye whiskey
Shake well, strain into a large glass and fill with seltzer water.

THE ART OF MAKING A COCKTAIL & MORE

BRANDY (de Cognac)

Glass of Domecq Tres Cepas
Teaspoon of sugar
An egg
Shake well with chipped ice and sprinkle with nutmeg.

BUSSE

Glass of sloe gin
An egg yolk
2 dashes of apricot brandy
1/2 teaspoon of sugar
Shake well with chipped ice, strain into a wine glass and sprinkle with nutmeg.

COFFEE (de Cafe)

1/2 glass Pedro Domecq Fundador Brandy
1/2 glass Port wine
An egg
Teaspoon of sugar
Shake well and sprinkle with nutmeg.

CHOCOLATE

1/2 glass Domecq Tres Cepas
1/2 glass sloe gin
An egg yolk
Teaspoon of sugar
Shake well with chipped ice.

CREAM (DE LECHE)

1 egg
3 glass of cream
Dashes of curaçao
Shake well with chipped ice and sprinkle with nutmeg.

EGG (DE HUEVO)

An egg
Teaspoon of sugar
Teaspoon of maraschino liqueur
Glass of milk
Shake and sprinkle with nutmeg.

GIN (DE GINEBRA)

Glass of English gin
An egg
Teaspoon of sugar
Shake well and strain.

PORT WINE (DE VINO OPORTO)

Glass of Port wine
An egg
Teaspoon of sugar
Shake, strain and sprinkle with nutmeg.

REVIVER (RESUCITADOR)

Glass of sloe gin
1/4 glass of curaçao
An egg
Shake well and sprinkle with nutmeg.

SHERRY (DE VINO DE JEREZ)
Glass of Jerez Domecq La Ina.
An egg
Teaspoon of sugar
Shake, strain and sprinkle with nutmeg.

THE ART OF MAKING A COCKTAIL & MORE

ABSINTHE (AJENJO)
1/2 glass of green absinthe
1/2 glass of water
Shake well with chipped ice.

ABSINTHE DRIP
Put the strainer over the crystal glass, ice well and pour a small cup of water slowly until the mixture is made with wormwood, and serve well shaken.

ASSORTED SHAKES (FRAPES SURTIDOS)
Put chipped ice into a cocktail glass and fill with
which ever cream you want, like:

Crème de Menthe
Curaçao
Chartreuse
Bénédictine
Anisette.

THE ART OF MAKING A COCKTAIL & MORE

AMER PICON
Glass of Amer Picon
1/2 glass of grenadine
Ice cubes and soda water.

BERMUDA
1/3 Domecq Tres Cepas
1/3 English gin
1/3 French vermouth
Ice cubes and soda water.

BOURBON
Glass of Bourbon whiskey
Ice cubes and soda water.

BRANDY (de Cognac)
Glass of Domecq Tres Cepas
Ice cubes. Fill with soda.

GIN (GINEBRA)
Glass of English gin
Ice cubes
Lemon peel and fill with soda.

IRISH ROSE (Rosa Irlandesa)
Glass of Irish whiskey
1/3 grenadine syrup
Fill with soda and stir.

PALL MALL
1/3 Domecq Tres Cepas
1/3 Italian vermouth
1/3 English gin
Ice cubes and fill with soda.

POMPIER (Bombero)
1/2 French vermouth
1/2 crème de cassis
Ice cubes and fill with soda.

RYE (de whiskey de centeno)
Glass of Rye whiskey
Ice cubes and fill with soda.

SCOTCH (de whiskey Escoces)
Glass of Scotch whisky
Ice cubes and fill with soda.

THE ART OF MAKING A COCKTAIL & MORE

BRANDY (Cognac)
2 teaspoons of syrup
Glass of Domecq Tres Cepas in a silver
glass or other, fill with chipped ice.
Stir slowly and add sprigs of mint. Serve with a straw.

GIN (Ginebra)
2 teaspoons of syrup
Glass of English gin in a silver cup or
other kind.
Chipped ice and sprigs of mint.
Serve with a straw.

GRAPE JUICE (de zumo de Uva)
Teaspoon of syrup
Half of 1/4 bottle of grape juice in a
silver cup or other kind.
Chipped ice, sprig of mint.
Serve with a straw.

KENTUCKY MINT
(de yerbabuena a lo Kentuckiano)
2 teaspoons of syrup
Glass of Bourbon whiskey in a silver cup with chipped ice. Stir slowly; take an ice pick and chip off the smalll pieces of ice adhering to the walls of the glass, carefully place a sprig of mint and serve with a straw.

MINT WESTERN STYLE
(DE YERBABUENA A LO OCCIDENTAL)

In a glass of lemonade, dissolve a lump of sugar with 3 sprigs of mint. Add chipped ice, a glass of Bourbon whiskey, 1/2 teaspoon of Cuban rum. Stir well, adorn with fruit, add a sprig of mint and serve.

THE ART OF MAKING A COCKTAIL & MORE

Ponches

ADALOR
A peach split with a fork.
1/2 bottle of champagne.

AMERICAN BEAUTY (BELLEZA AMERICANA)
Teaspoon of crème de menthe in a glass
with chipped ice.
Add juice of 1/2 orange
1/2 teaspoon of sugar
1/2 glass of Pedro Domecq Fundador Brandy
1/2 glass of French vermouth
Shake, strain into a glass decorated with fruit and add a teaspoon of Port.

ARCTIC (ARTICO)
Glass of raspberry syrup
Juice of 2 lemons
2 1/2 bottles of ginger ale
1/2 bottle of cold English tea
Decorate with fruit and mint.

ASTOR PUNCH (PONCHE ASTOR)
1/2 glass of white crème de menthe
Chopped ice in a glass
Add 1/2 glass of sloe gin
Decorate with fruit.

BILL MEYER PUCH

Dashes of lemon
Lump of sugar
2 slices of pineapple
2 orange peels
1 lemon peel
Use a large glass with 5 pieces of ice, fill with Champagne, stir well, add cherries and serve.

BISHOP PUNCH (Jarra)

Juice of 1/2 lemon
Glass of syrup
Glass of Cuban rum
1/2 bottle of red wine (for 2 or 3 people)
Decorate with fruit and mint.

BLACKSTONE NECTAR

Juice of a small orange
Juice of a small lemon
Raspberry syrup to taste.
Shake, strain into a glass with a little ice, fill with seltzer and decorate with fruit and sprigs of mint.

BRANDY-MILK PUNCH
(Ponche de cognac y leche)

Glass of Pedro Domecq Fundador Brandy
Dashes of Cuban rum
Teaspoon of sugar
Fill with milk, shake, strain and add a little nutmeg.

BRANDY PUNCH (Ponche de cognac)

Crushed ice
Glass of Domecq cognac
A little sugar
2 dashes of raspberry syrup
Dash of marachino liqueur
Stir well, add seltzer water and adorn with mint.

BORDELAISE PUNCH (Ponche bordalesa)

Juice of 1/2 lemon
2 dashes raspberry syrup
Teaspoon of sugar
Glass of kirschwasser in a glass with chipped ice
2 lemon peels
2 orange peels
Stir well and fill with a little seltzer water.

BOSTON MILK PUNCH (Ponche de leche Boston)

1/2 glass of American whiskey
1/2 glass of Cuban rum
Teaspoon of sugar
1/2 bottle of milk
Shake and serve.

BOURBON WHISKEY PUNCH
RYE WHISKEY PUNCH
Juice of 1/2 lemon
Teaspoon of sugar
Glass of Rye or Bourbon whiskey
Shake, strain into a fine glass with ice and decorate with fruit.

BRUNSWICK PUNCH
Like a Milk Shake, but without the sugar and using raspberry syrup in place of 1/2 glass of curaçao.
Adorn with fruit and mint.

BULLS EYE (OJO DE TORO)
1/2 bottle of cider
1/2 bottle of clear Polar beer
Glass of Domecq cognac
Garnish with chopped fruit.

BURGUNDY (BORGONA)
Use a large bowl in which you place;
Glass of Pedro Domecq Fundador Brandy
A glass of dark curaçao
Glass of maraschino liqueur
1 liter of Burgundy wine
1/2 bottle of carbonated mineral water
Chipped ice
Stir well and adorn with 5 pieces of pineapple, cherries and a sprig of mint.

BULL MOOSE PUNCH
1/3 Rye whiskey
1/3 Bourbon whiskey
1/3 English gin
Dash of Angostura Bitters
2 dashes of syrup
Shake, strain into a glass with chipped ice and garnish with fruit.

CARDINAL PUNCH
Put into a punch bowl two liters of carbonated mineral water, 2 liters red wine, 1/2 bottle of cognac Domeeq, 1/2 bottle of Cuban rum, 1/2 bottle of sparkling Moselle wine sparkling, glass of Italian vermouth, three sliced oranges; 1/4 of a pineapple slices, and a large piece of ice, and serve in punch cups.

CHAMPAGNE ADONIS
Use a crystal punch bowl.
Glass of Pedro Domecq Fundador Brandy
Glass of maraschino liqueuro
Glass of yellow Chartreuse
Glass of syrup
A large piece of ice
1 liter of Champagne
1/2 bottle of carbonated mineral water
A small lemon cut into pieces
An orange
6 pieces of pineapple
Cherries and a sprig of mint
Stir well and add a little sugar.

CHAMPAGNE EXTRA

Use a crystal punch bowl.
Glass of Pedro Domecq Fundador Brandy
Glass of white curaçao
Glass of maraschino liqueur
Glass of syrup
Juice of 1/2 lemon
Liter of Champagne
1/2 bottle of carbonated mineral water
A large piece of ice
2 slices of cucumber
An orange cut into pieces
A lemon in pieces
4 or 5 pieces of pineapple
6 cherries
2 pieces of pear
Sprig of mint
Stir well and serve in a Delmonico glass.

CHAMPAGNE POLAR
(A ONE GALLON PUNCH BOWL)

1 liter of Champagne
6 1/2 bottles of Polar been
1 liter of Apollinaris
1 liter of lemon juice
2 glasses of Curaçao
A glass of apple jack
A glass of Pedro Domecq Fundador Brandy cognac
Sugar to taste and adorn with fruit.

CHAMPAGNE PUNCH
(Ponche de Champagne)
A one gallon punch bowl.
Juice of 4 lemons
Glass of maraschino liqueur
3 glasses of Pedro Domecq Fundador Brandy
Dashes of yellow Chartreuse
2 liters of Champagne
2 liters of Apollinaris or other mineral water
Sweeten with sugar to taste and decorate with fruit.

CHAMPAGNE PUNCH No. 2
A one gallon punch bowl
2 liters of Champagne
1 liter of Rhine wine
1 liter of Apollinaris
1 liter of lemon juice
2 glasses of curaçao
Glass of apple jack
Glass of Pedro Domecq Fundador Brandy cognac
Sweeten with sugar to taste and decorate with fruit.

CLARET PUNCH No. 1
A one gallon punch bowl
Juice of 6 lemons
2 glasses of curaçao
4 glass of Domecq Tres Cepas cognac
2 dashes of Bénédictine
2 liters of red wine
2 liters of Apollinaris
Sweeten with sugar to taste and decorate with fruit.

CLARET PUNCH No. 2
A small glass and chipped ice
Glass of red wine
4 dashes of lemon juice
2 dashes of Curaçao
2 dashes of syrup
Decorate with fruit.

CLARET PUNCH No. 3
Use a large crystal bowl in which you put:
1 lemon cut into pieces
1 orange cut into pieces
5 slices of pineapple
Glass of curaçao
Glass of Pedro Domecq Fundador Brandy
Glass of syrup
Dash of maraschino liqueur
Dash of lemon
6 or 8 cherries
A liter of red wine
Bottle of soda or a similar type of carbonated water
Sprig of mint.

COMBINATION PUNCH
Juice of 1/2 lemon
Juice of 1/2 orange
Glass of Rye whiskey or Bourbon
Shake, strain into a glass with ice and decorate with fruit.

CONCLAVE
Juice of an orange
Glass of raspberry syrup
Teaspoon of sugar
3 glasses of fresh milk
Shake, strain into a fine glass and serve.

CREAM PUNCH (Ponche crema)
Teaspoon of sugar
1/2 glass of Domecq Tres Cepas
1/2 glass of maraschino liqueur
Bottle of whole sweet milk
Dashes of Curaçao
Shake and strain into a punch glass

CREOLE PUNCH (Ponche criolla)
Glass of French red wine
1/2 glass of Domecq Tres Cepas
2 dashes of apricot brandy
Dashes of Cuban rum
Teaspoon of syrup
Put chipped ice into a glass and adorn with fruit.
You could also serve hot with spice and a lemon peel.

CUBAN MILK PUNCH
(Ponche de leche a la Cubana)
Glass of vanilla
An egg
Teaspoon of sugar
3 glasses of fresh milk
Shake, strain and serve in a fine glass.

CURAÇAO PUNCH

Juice of 1/4 lemon
Sugar to taste
3/4 glass of curaçao
1/4 glass of Domecq Tres Cepas
Shake, strain into a glass with chipped ice and decorate with fruit.

ELMWOOD PUNCH

4 half bottles of grape juice
1/2 bottle of red wine
1/2 bottle of Champagne
2 teaspoons of grated pineapple
Sugar to taste
Adorn with fruit.

EMPRESS PUNCH (Ponche Emperatariz)

2 lumps of sugar dissolved
3 dashes of Angostura Bitters
5 pieces of ice
1/4 liter of Champagne
Adorn with fruit, sprigs of mint and 2 pieces of lemon.

FISH HOUSE PUNCH (Ponche pescaderia)

For one person:
Juice of 1/2 lemon
2/3 Cuban rum
1/3 Domecq Tres Cepas cognac
Dashes of peach brandy
1/2 teaspoon of sugar
Shake, strain into a glass with chipped ice and adorn with fruit.

FISH HOUSE PUNCH (EN CONSERVA)
Juice of 4 lemons
1 1/2 pounds of granulated sugar
1/2 bottle of curaçao
1/2 bottle of Cuban rum
1/2 bottle of Bénédictine
1 liter of peach brandy
4 liters of Bourbon whiskey

Place these ingredients into a jar without a lid for 10 days, stirring once during that period. At the end of that time, strain into a punch bowl, adding a liter of Champagne and a liter of carbonated mineral water for every 3 liters of punch.

"GARCIA MIER"
A teaspoon of sugar
Glass of Jerez La Ina
An egg
3 glasses of milk
Dashes of Domecq cognac
Shake, strain into a fine glass and serve.

GIN PUNCH (Ponche de ginebra)
Juice of 1/2 lemon
Teaspoon of sugar
Glass of Dutch gin
A glass with crushed ice
Shake, strain and adorn with fruit.

GINGER ALE (SIN LICORES)

(Para 6 personas. - Jarra de cristal)
Juice of 3 lemons
Juice of 3 oranges
2 glasses of grenadine
Sugar to taste
Shake well and strain into a punch bowl
Add a liter of ginger ale
Large pieces of ice
Adorn with fruit of the season and mint.

GINGER ALE

(Para 6 personas - Jarra de cristal)
Glass of Pedro Domecq Fundador Brandy
1/2 glass of maraschino liqueur
Dashes of Bénédictine
3 1/2 bottles of ginger ale
Large pieces of ice
4 or 5 pieces of orange
4 or 5 slices of pineapple
4 or 5 pieces of lemon
Sprigs of mint
Add sugar
Stir well and serve in fine glasses.

GOODMAN PUNCH

Juice of 1/2 lemon
1/4 Jerez La Ina
3/4 Rye whiskey
1/2 teaspoon of sugar
Shake, strain and decorate with fruit.

GRAPE JUICE (Zumo de Uva)
(Para 6 personas - Jarra grande)
Glass of Pedro Domecq Fundador Brandy
Glass of maraschino liqueur
Glass of yellow Chartreuse
Dash of grenadine
Juice of 1/2 lemon
Large pieces of ice
A liter of grape juice
1/2 bottle of Apollinaris
Garnish with fruit and mint.

GRAPE JUICE (sin licores)
Juice of 2 lemons
Juice of 2 oranges
2 glasses of grenadine
Shake and strain into a crystal punch bowl
Large pieces of ice
A liter of red or white grape juice
1/2 bottle of Apollinaris
Regular amount of sugar
Decorate with fruit and mint, stirring well with a large spoon.

HARDING PUNCH
Use a 2 gallon punch bowl.
Liter of Cuban rum
Liter of Domecq Tres Cepas
Liter of Champagne
2/3l liter of palm wine
Liter of peach brandy
3 pounds of granulated sugar
1/8 pound of green tea, brewed
2 liters of ice water

HERALD PUNCH

2 glasses of orange juice
Glass of American whiskey
Glass with crushed ice
Adorn with fruit and add dashes of Cuban rum.

IRISH WHISKEY PUNCH
(PONCHE DE WHISKEY IRLANDES)

Juice of 1/2 lemon
Teaspoon of sugar
Glass of Irish whiskey
Shake and strain into a glass with crushed ice. Adorn with fruit.

KNICKERBOCKER PUNCH

Juice of 1/2 lemon
Teaspoon of sugar
Glass of Cuban rum
Shake, strain into a glass with crushed ice, adorn with fruit and add a little red wine.

LORD BALTIMORE

Juice of 2 lemons
Teaspoon of sugar
Glass of Scotch whisky
2 dashes of Bénédictine
Shake, strain into a glass and decorate with fruit.

LORD LATOUNNE
Use a crystal punch bowl
A thin lemon peel
2 glasses of Jerez La Ina
Mint leaves
6 cherries
Liter of red wine
1/2 bottle of lemonade.

MERRY WIDOW
Juice of 1/2 lemon
1/2 teaspoon of sugar
Glass of sloe gin
Dashes of vanilla
Shake, strain into a glass with crushed ice and add a teaspoon of milk.

MILK (DE LECHE)
Teaspoon of sugar
2/3 Bourbon whiskey
1/3 French vermouth
Dashes of Cuban rum
A half glass of fresh milk
Shake well, strain into a large glass and sprinkle a little nutmeg.

MILLIONAIRE (MILLONARIO)
Juice of 1 lemon
Teaspoon of sugar
Glass of Scotch whisky
2 dashes of grenadine
Shake well, strain into a glass, adorn with fruit and add dashes of white crème de menthe.

MONTICELLO

1/2 bottle of Champagne
Glass of Domecq cognac
Juice of 1/2 lemon
Sugar to taste and decorate with fruit.

MOSELLE WINE (Vino Mosela)

Glass of Pedro Domecq Fundador Brandy
Glass of maraschino liqueur
Dashes of yellow Chartreuse
Dashes of Bénédictine
Liter of Mosel wine
1/2 bottle of Apollinaris
Large pieces of ice
8 cherries or grapes
1 lemon in pieces
1 orange in pieces
2 or 3 slices of pineapple
Sprigs of mint
Stir well and serve in Delmonico glasses.

MILK SHAKE

1/2 teaspoon of sugar
1/2 bottle of fresh milk
Dash of raspberry syrup
Shake well.

MINT (YERBABUENA)

Sprigs of very green mint
In a tall glass, a piece of ice and
1/2 bottle of ginger ale.

NECTAR POLAR

Use a crystal bowl.
1/2 bottle of Champagne
1/2 bottle of Polar clear beer
1 glass of Chartreuse.

PEACH BRANDY
(DE AGUARIENTE DE MELOCOTON)

Juice of 1/2 lemon
Teaspoon of sugar
Glass of peach brandy
Shake, strain into a glass with shaved ice and adorn with fruit. Stir well and serve in a Delmonico glass.

PIÑA

Juice of 2 oranges
Glass of raspberry liqueur
Glass of maraschino liqueur
Glass of Old Tom gin
Liter of Moselle wine
A pineapple in pieces
Ice
Serve with a straw in a fine glass.

POLAR

Juice of 1/2 orange
Juice of 1/2 lemon
Grenadine to taste
Shake, strain into a glass with chipped ice, add 1/2 Polar Clara, and adorn with fruit and a sprig of mint.

PONY

Juice of 6 lemons
Juice of 1/2 pineapple
Liter of Bourbon whiskey
Liter of green tea
1/2 bottle of Cuban rum
1/2 bottle of maraschino liqueur
Blend very well and serve in a punch glass decorated with fruit.

REGENT

A lemon in pieces
An orange in pieces
A tin of canned pineapple
1/4 bottle of Cuban rum
1/4 bottle of American whiskey
18 lumps of sugar
Blend together in a punch bowl, keep for 2 hours in a cold place. Later add a half bottle of tea an stir slowly. When it is ready to serve, place the punch bowl on the table and add a liter of Champagne.

RHINE WINE (DE VINO DEL RHIN)

Use a one gallon punch bowl.
Juice of 8 lemons
2 glasses pf Pedro Domecq Fundador Brandy
2 glass of curaçao
A glass of Bénédictine
2 liters of Rhine wine
2 liters of carbonated water
Sugar to taste.

RHINE WINE (VINO DEL RHIN)

Use a large crystal bowl.
Glass of Pedro Domecq Fundador Brandy
1/2 glass of maraschino liqueur
1/2 glass of Bénédictine
Dashes of curaçao
Large pieces of ice
1/2 bottle of Apollinaris
Liter of Rhine wine
4 pieces of lemon
6 pieces of orange
6 pieces of pineapple
4 pieces of pear
8 cherries
Dashes of lemon juice
Stir well and decorate with a sprig of mint.

ROMAN (A LA ROMANA)

Juice of 1/2 lemon
1/2 glass of water
Teaspoon of sugar
1/4 glass of Cuban rum
1/4 glass of dark curaçao
Shake well and strain into a glass adorned with fruit. To finish add a little Domecq cognac into each glass before serving.

EL ARTE DE HACER UN COCKTAIL Y ALGO MAS

ROOSEVELT

1/2 lemon peeled
Teaspoon of sugar
Glass of Apple jack
1/2 glass of water

Shake, strain into a glass adorned with fruit. Before serving add a little Domecq cognac to each glass.

RUM (DE RON)

Juice of 1/2 lemon
Teaspoon of sugar
Glass of Cuban rum
Dashes of Domecq cognac

Shake, strain into a glass adorned with fruit.

SABROSOS

Use a large crystal bowl into which you put:
A lemon cut into pieces
An orange cut into pieces
5 slices of pineapple
Glass of curaçao
Glass of Pedro Domecq Fundador Brandy
Glass of syrup
2 glass of crème de menthe
Dash of maraschino liqueur
Dash of lemon
6 to 8 cherries
6 bottles of clear Polar Beer
Bottle of soda or carbonated water
Sprigs of mint

SALOME
Teaspoon of sugar
An egg
Glass of curaçao
1/2 bottle of milk
Shake and strain into a glass.

SAUTERNES
Juice of 5 lemons
2 glasses of Pedro Domecq Fundador Brandy cognac
Glass of apple jack
Glass of pineapple juice
2 dashes of yellow Chartreuse.
2 liters of Sauterne wine
1 liter of Apollinaris water
Sugar to taste and adorn with fruit.

SAUTERNES CUP
A large crystal bowl.
Glass of Pedro Domecq Fundador Brandy
Glass of yellow Chartreuse
Glass of French maraschino liqueur
Large pieces of ice
1/2 bottle of Apollinaris
Liter of Sauterne
Juice of 1/2 lemon
5 pieces of orange
4 slices of pineapple
2 pieces of cucumber peel
6 cherries
Sprigs of mint.

SAUTERNES (AL ESTILO DEL SUR)
Use a large crystal punch bowl
Glass of lemon juice
1/2 glass of Pedro Domecq Fundador Brandy
1/2 glass of curaçao
1/2 glass of Bénédictine
Large pieces of ice
Liter of Sauterne
1/2 lemon in pieces
1/2 orange in pieces
5 slices of pineapple
Cherries
1/2 bottle of Apollinaris
Stir well and add sprigs of mint.

SCHLEY
Juice and peel of a lemon
Teaspoon of sugar
1/3 glass of Cuban rum
2/3 glass of Rye or Bourbon whiskey
Shake, strain into a glass with shaved ice, garnish with fruit and mint.

SCOTCH WHISKY (DE WHISKEY ESCOCES)
Juice of 1/2 lemon
Teaspoon of sugar
Glass of Scotch whisky
Shake, strain into a glass and decorate with fruit.

SHERIDAN
Lemonade with 1/2 glass of American whiskey.

SIDRA CUP (Cider)
Use a large crystal bowl in which you put:
4 pieces of lemon
5 pieces of orange
5 slices of pineapple
Glass of Pedro Domecq Fundador Brandy
1/2 glass of curaçao
1/2 glass of maraschino liqueur
1 liter of sparkling cider or natural,
whichever you prefer
2 dashes of lemon juice
Cherries
Large piece of ice
Sprig of mint.

SIDRA CUP (Sin Licores)
Use a large crystal bowl
Juice of 2 lemons
Juice of an orange
Glass of grenadine
Glass of syrup
Large piece of ice
3 or 4 pieces of lemon
4 slices of pineapple
4 pieces of orange
2 pieces of cucumber peel
6 cherries
A liter of cider champagne
Stir well with a large spoon, add sprigs of mint and serve in a Delmonico glass.

EL ARTE DE HACER UN COCKTAIL Y ALGO MAS

SIDRA POLAR

3 bottles of cider
6 1/2 bottles of Polar
Liter of Apollinaris
Liter of lemon juice
2 glasses of curaçao
Glass of apple jack
Glass of Pedro Domecq Fundador Brandy cognac
Sugar to taste and adorn with fruit.

SOOTHER

Juice of 1/2 lemon
Teaspoon of sugar
1/4 Domecq cognac
1/4 Cuban rum
1/4 apple jack
1/4 curaçao
Shake, strain into a glass of chipped ice and decorate with fruit.

SPECIAL

Glass of orange juice
Glass of lemon juice
glass of English gin
1/2 glass of syrup.
Shake, strain into a glass with ice and serve.

STEINWAY
Juice of a lemon
Teaspoon of sugar
Glass of Scotch whisky
1/2 glass of water
Shake, strain into a punch glass and fill with seltzer water.

TURK'S NECK
1/2 bottle of Champagne
1/2 of French red wine
Large piece of ice
Adorn with fruit and mint.

VELVET
In a crystal bowl
1/2 bottle of Champagne
1/2 bottle of dark Polar beer
Large piece of ice.

WALDORF
Juice of an orange
Juice of a lemon
An egg.
Shake strain and fill the glass with seltzer water.

WALDORF EXTRA

Juice of 1/2 lemon
Teaspoon of sugar
Glass of American whiskey
1/2 glass of water.
Shake, strain into a glass with crushed ice, adorn with fruit and add a little red wine.

WHISKEY (A LA ANTIGUA)

Liter of Bourbon whiskey
3 glasses of lemon juice
3 glasses of curaçao
1/2 bottle of carbonated mineral water
Glass of syrup
Large piece of ice
3 or 4 slices of cucumber peel
Decorate with fruit and mint.

AMERICAN GROG
A lump of sugar
1/2 lemon juice
Glass of Cuban rum
Fill the glass with hot water.

BLUE BLAZER (LLAMARADA AZUL)
Use a cup of thick glass or metal
1/2 lump of sugar
Fill 2/3 of the cup with hot water
Add Rye whiskey to the rest.
Apply a lit match and rotate the glass 3 or 4 times, squeeze a lemon and serve.

CAFE BOULES
Rub the rim of a cocktail glass all around with a lemon peel. Dust with powdered sugar.
7/8 hot coffee
1/8 Pedro Domecq Fundador Brandy or Tres Cepas cognac
Ignite and serve.

CARIBE
2 lumps of sugar
2 dashes Angostura bitters
Glass of apple juice
Squeeze a lemon peel, add a little hot water, light with a match and serve.

COLON
1/2 lump of sugar
Glass of American whiskey
Lemon peel and fill glass with hot water.

COGNAC QUEMADO CON MELOCOTON
Heat a glass of Pedro Domecq Fundador Brandy cognac with a lump of sugar in a saucer. Put several pieces of dried peach in a thick glass and pour in the hot liquid.

CRIOLLO
2 teaspoons of syrup
2 dashes of Cuban rum
Dash of Hungarian apricot brandy
Glass of French red wine
Teaspoon of spice
Lemon peel
Heat until almost boiling.

HOT AMERICAN GROG
2 teaspoons of syrup
2 dashes of Cuban rum
Dash of Hungarian apricot brandy
Glass of French red wine
Teaspoon of spices
Lemon peel
Heat until almost boiling.

HOT APPLEJACK TODDY
1/2 lump of sugar
Glass of apple juice in a thick glass
Lemon peel
Fill with hot water.

HOT CLARET PUNCH
(PONCHE CALIENTE DE VINO TINTO)
Juice of 1/2 lemon
Teaspoon of sugar
Cinnamon to taste
Glass of Claret wine
Lemon peel
Heat to boiling, strain into a thick crystal glass and serve.

HOT LEMONADE (LIMONADA CALIENTE)
Juice of 1 lemon
Teaspoon of sugar
Fill with hot water
Stir and add lemon peel.

HOT MILK PUNCH
Glass of Scotch whisky
2 teaspoons of sugar
Dash of Cuban rum
Fill with hot milk.
Stir and serve.

HOT SPICED RUM
1/2 lump of sugar
Glass of Cuban rum
1/2 teaspoon of spices
Fill with hot water.

MULL CLARET
Lump of sugar
2 dashes of lemon juice
Dash of Angostura Bitters
2 glasses of red wine
Teaspoon of spices

Put a red hot poker into the liquid until it is very hot. Ladle the liquid only into mugs or glasses and serve.

PORT WINE NEGUS
1/2 lump of sugar
2/3 glass of hot water
Glass of Port wine
Stir and add grated nutmeg.

TOM AND JERRY
Take several egg whites and beat until frothy. Add 1 1/2 teaspoons of sugar per egg white. Beat the yolks separately. Stir the yolks and whites together until a thick paste is formed. Add as much bicarbonate as the size of a nickel and continue beating so that the eggs will not separate.

To serve: Put a teaspoon of paste into a glass, a glass of Cuban rum and Domecq cognac blended and fill with hot water or hot milk and add grated nutmeg. Stir and serve.

Retrescos

AMER PICON POUFFLE
3/4 glass of Amer Picon
1/4 glass grenadine syrup
White of an egg
Shake, strain and fill the glass with seltzer water.

ANGOSTURA GINGER ALE
Glass of ginger ale
3 dashes of Angostura bitters.

ANGOSTURA PHOSPHATE
1/2 teaspoon of phosphate acid
Teaspoon of Angostura Bitters
2 teaspoons of lemon juice
Sweetened juice of 1/2 lemon
Fill the glass with carbonated water.

ANGOSTURA SODA
Large glass with three pieces of ice
5 or 6 dashes of Angostura Bitters
2 pieces of orange
Fill the glass with lemonade and add sugar to taste.

ARDSLEY
A piece of ice
Glass of Old Tom gin
Medium bottle of ginger ale
Sprig of mint.

AUTOMOBILE
Glass of English gin
Medium bottle of ginger ale
Sprig of mint
A large piece of ice.

BEER SHANDY
1/2 Trimalta
1/2 clear Polar beer.

BILLY TAYLOR
Glass of English gin
Juice of 1/2 lemon
Bottle of soda
Piece of ice.

BLACKSTONE
Lemon peel
Glass of Cuban rum
Bottle of soda.

BOSTON
Juice of 1/2 lemon
Teaspoon of sugar
Glass of Cuban rum
Bottle of soda.

BULL
Juice of 1/2 lemon
1/2 water
1/2 clear Polar beer
Sugar
Piece of ice.

BULL POLAR
Orange peel
Juice of an orange
Piece of ice
Glass of English gin
1/2 water
1/2 Polar extra dark beer
Sugar.

CHAMPOLA DE GUANABANA
Juice of soursop
1/2 glass of milk
Teaspoon of sugar
Shake in a cocktail shaker. Serve in a large glass.

CHAMPOLA DE ANON
Juice of an anonna
1/2 glass of milk
Teaspoon of sugar
Shake in a cocktail shaker. Serve in a large glass.

CHIQUITICA
1/2 glass of grenadine
1/2 bottle of soda
Condensed milk "Lechera"
Chipped ice
Shake in the same glass.

CHOCOLATE CREAM SODA
Glass of Chocolate cream
A little syrup
Serve in a large glass and fill with soda.

COUNTRY CLUB
1/2 glass of grenadine
1/2 glass of French vermouth
Bottle of soda
Chipped ice

DUNHAM
Large orange peel
Glass of orange juice
Glass of Bourbon or Rye whiskey
1/2 bottle of ginger ale
Ice cubes
Stir slowly.

DURKEE
A lemon peeled
Teaspoon of sugar
Glass of Jamaican Cuban rum
Bottle of soda.

EGG PHOSPHATE
A egg
Teaspoon of sugar
Juice of an orange
3 dashes of phosphate acid
1/2 of carbonated water
Shake, strain and serve with a straw.

ENSALADA
Large glass of ice
Glass of grenadine
Adorn with pieces of pineapple and orange and fill with soda or mineral water.

FLORODORA
Juice of 1/2 lemon
1/4 glass of raspberry syrup
1/4 glass of English gin
1/2 bottle of ginger ale
Ice cubes.

FLORODORA (Estil Imperial)
Juice of 1/2 lemon
Glass of Pedro Domecq Fundador Brandy
1/2 bottle of ginger ale

GAMBRINUS
1/2 bottle of Trimalta
Yolk of an egg
Shake well.

GINGER ALE
Lemon peel cut into a spiral.
Put a piece of ice in the center of the spiral and add 1/2 bottle of ginger ale.

GRAPE JUICE (Zumo de uva)
Lemon peel
1/4 bottle of red or white grape juice
Piece of ice
Bottle of soda.

HAWAII
Peel and juice of an orange
Glass of Rye whiskey
1/2 bottle of ginger ale.

HABANA
Lemon peel
Piece of ice
Glass of Cuban rum
1/2 bottle of soda.

ICE CREAM SODA
Glass of ice cream
A little syrup
A large glass filled with soda.

IRISH WHISKEY (Whiskey Escocés)
Lemon peel
A glass of Scotch whisky
Bottle of soda
Dash of Angostura Bitters

KDT
A large glass. A whiskey rickey with a quarter Ginger Ale and fill the glass with seltzer water.

KIKI
1/2 teaspoon of sugar
Juice of 1/2 lemon
Juice of 1/2 orange
A glass filled to the mid-point with crushed ice

KHATURA
1/4 glass of French vermouth
1/4 glass of Italian vermouth
1/2 glass of English gin
2 dashes of Angostura Bitters
Bottle of soda.

LEMON PHOSPHATE
2 dashes of phosphate acid
Teaspoon of lemon juice
1/2 of lemon soda.

LEMONADES

LIMONADA ANGOSTURA
Add a teaspoon of Angostura Bitters to each glass of lemonade.

LIMONADA APOLLINARIS
Juice of 1 lemon
Teaspoon of sugar
1/4 Apollinaris
Stir well and decorate with fruit.
Serve with a straw.

LIMONADA DE VINO TINTO
Add a little red wine to a lemonade.

LIMONADA CLUB SODA
A teaspoon of sugar
Juice of 1 lemon
1/4 club soda
Stir and decorate with fruit.

LIMONADA EGG (DE HUEVO)
Juice of 1 lemon
Teaspoon of sugar
An egg
Add chipped ice and water
Stir well.

LIMONADA FRUIT
(DE FRUTAS)
Add pieces of pineapple, orange, cherries and other fruits of the season to lemonade.

LIMONADA NARANJADA
Juice of one orange
Juice of 1/2 lemon
1/2 teaspoon of sugar
Fill the glass with ice and distilled water.
Adorn with fruit and serve.

LIMONADA CON AGUA DE SELTZ
Juice of a lemon
Teaspoon of sugar
Fill glass halfway with ice
Fill with seltzer water and adorn with fruit.

LIMONADA CON GASEOSA
Juice of a lemon
Teaspoon of sugar
Glass half filled with ice
Bottle of soda
Stir slowly and adorn with fruit.

LIMONADA CON WHISKEY
Lemonade, add a little Scotch whisky and adorn with fruit.

MAZAGRAN
A large glass with ice
A measure of coffee
Teaspoon of sugar
1/4 of squeezed lemon
Fill with water and serve.

MINT (Yerbabuena)
A bunch of green mint which has been squeezed a little
A piece of ice
1/2 bottle of ginger ale

MORA
2 glasses of Rhine wine
1/2 peeled lemon
Lemon peel
Piece of ice
1/3 glass of curaçao
Bottle of soda

NARRAGANSETT
Peel and juice of an orange
Glass of Bourbon whiskey
1/2 bottle of ginger ale.

NARANJA MAMBI

2 glasses of orange juice
Glass of English gin
Teaspoon of sugar
A large glass.
Chipped ice
Fill glass with seltzer water and adorn with fruit.

POLAR

Peel of a lemon cut thin
1/2 bottle of clear Polar beer
Sugar and ice.

PORT WINE SANGAREE (SANGRIA OF PORT WINE)

1/2 teaspoon of sugar
Glass of Port wine
A little water, stir with a spoon and add grated nutmeg.

REMSEN

Lemon peel
Glass of English gin
Bottle of soda.

RHINE WINE AND SELTZER
A glass half filled with seltzer water.
Fill with Rhine wine and serve.

ROBERT E. LEE
Dash of absinthe
Juice of 1/2 lemon
Glass of Scotch whisky
1/2 bottle of ginger ale.

SABBATH (Sabatino)
1/2 glass of Domecq cognac
1/2 glass of Italian vermouth
Juice of 1/2 lemon
Bottle of soda and adorn with 3 sprigs of mint.

SANGAREE POLAR
(Sangria de Cerveza Polar)
Fill a glass with clear Polar beer, add a teaspoon of sugar, stir slowly and add grated nutmeg.

SANGAREE SHERRY
(Sangria de vino Jerez)
Prepare the same as Port Wine Sangaree, using Jerez Domecq La Ina in place of Port wine.

SCOTCH (Escocés)
Lemon peel
3 pieces of ice in a large glass
Glass of Scotch whisky
Bottle of soda.

SEA SIDE (Orilla del mar)
Juice of a lemon
Glass of Grenadine syrup

UZCUDUM
1/2 Trimalta
1/2 clear Polar beer
1 egg
Shake and serve in a large glass.

WHITE (Blanco)
Juice of 1/2 orange
1/2 glass of Scotch whisky
Dash of Angostura Bitters
A bottle of ginger ale
Serve in a large glass.

ZARZAPARRILLA
3 or 4 pieces of lemon
Juice of 1/2 lemon
Piece of ice 1/2 bottle of Zarzaparrilla

THE ART OF MAKING A COCKTAIL & MORE

GIN (DE GINEBRA)

Juice of 1/2 lemon
Piece of ice
Serve each the amount of English gin they want and fill the glass with seltzer water, stirring with a spoon.

IRISH WHISKEY
BOURBON OR RYE WHISKEY
SCOTCH WHISKY
RUM
COGNAC
APRICOT BRANDY

Make these like the Gin Rickey, using the spirits they want.

GIN BUCK

This is the same as the Gin Rickey using Ginger Ale in place of Seltzer water.

PORTO RICO (PUERTO RICO)

A Gin Rickey made with two dashes of raspberry syrup.

THE ART OF MAKING A COCKTAIL & MORE

BRANDY
A sugar cube in a large glass.
Glass of Domecq cognac
Ice cubes

GIN
A sugar cube in a large glass
Glass of English gin
lemon peel
Crushed ice and stir

IRISH
Dissolve a lump of sugar
Glass of Irish whiskey
2 small pieces of ice

RUM
Lump of sugar in a large glass
Glass of Cuban rum
Ice cubes

SCOTCH
A sugar cube dissolved in a large glass
Glass of Scotch whisky
Orange peel
Ice cubes

WHISKEY
Dissolve a sugar cube
Glass of Bourbon whiskey

THE ART OF MAKING A COCKTAIL & MORE

BRANDY
Dissolve 1/2 lump of sugar
3 sprigs of mint
Glass of Domecq cognac
Ice cubes
Stir and serve.

GIN
The same as Brandy Smash, using gin in place of cognac.

MINT
Squeeze a little mint and 1/2 sugar cube in a large glass
Glass of Scotch whisky
Ice cubes
Stir and serve.

WHISKEY
The same as Mint, using American whiskey.

THE ART OF MAKING A COCKTAIL & MORE

AMER PICON
Juice of 1/2 lemon
Teaspoon of sugar
1/4 grenadine
3/4 Amer Picon
Shake well, strain into a sour glass, adding pieces of orange and pineapple, and a cherry.

BRANDY
Juice of 1/2 lemon
1/2 teaspoon of sugar
Glass of Domecq Tres Cepas
Shake and strain. Adorn with fruit.

BRUNSWICK
Juice of a small lemon
Teaspoon of sugar
Glass of American whiskey
Shake well, strain and add a little red wine with the same fruit as the Amer Picon.

CANADIAN WHISKEY
Juice of 1/2 lemon
Teaspoon of sugar
Glass of Canadian whiskey
Shake well and garnish with fruit.

CHAMPAGNE
Juice of 1/2 lemon
Cube of sugar dissolved
Fill with champagne
Stir well and garnish with fruit.

DOUBLE STANDARD
Juice of a lemon
1/2 teaspoon of sugar
1/2 American whiskey
1/2 English gin
2 dashes of raspberry syrup
Shake, strain and add a little seltzer water.

EGG
Teaspoon of sugar
Juice of 1/2 lemon
Yolk of an egg
Dash of anisette
Glass of Pedro Domecq Fundador Brandy
Shake.

GIN
Juice of a small lemon
Teaspoon of sugar
Glass of English gin or whatever you
prefer more
Shake, strain into a medium glass and garnish with fruit.

GRENADINE
Juice of a small lemon
1/2 glass of grenadine
Glass of Bourbon whiskey
Shake well, strain into a medium glass and adorn with fruit.

GRENADINE-GIN
Juice of 1/2 lemon
1/3 grenadine
Glass of English gin
Shake well, strain into a glass and garnish with fruit.

HANCOCK
Juice of a lemon
Teaspoon of sugar
Glass of Bourbon whiskey
Dashes of Cuban rum
Shake, strain, adorn with fruit and add a little seltzer water.

IRISH WHISKEY
The same as a Whiskey Sour using Irish whiskey in place of Rye or Bourbon.

JERSEY
Juice of a lemon
Teaspoon of sugar
Glass of apple jack
Shake, strain, squeeze a lemon peel and garnish with fruit.

MILLIONAIRE

Juice of a lemon
1/3 grenadine
2/3 American whiskey
4 dashes of curaçao
Shake well and garnish with fruit.

ROOSEVELT

Juice of 1/2 lemon
Glass of apple jack
Teaspoon of sugar
Shake well and adorn with fruit.

RUM

Juice of a lemon
Teaspoon of sugar
Glass of Cuban rum
Dashes of curaçao
Shake, strain and garnish with fruit.

SARATOGA

Juice of 1/2 lemon
Teaspoon of sugar
1/4 Cuban rum
1/4 Domecq Tres Cepas
1/4 curaçao
1/4 apple jack
Shake well, strain, garnish with fruit and add a little red wine.

SCOTCH
The same as RUM, using Scotch whisky in place of Cuban rum.

SILVER
Juice of a lemon
Teaspoon of sugar
1/4 Cuban rum
1/4 Domecq Tres Cepas cognac
1/4 curaçao
1/4 apple jack
Shake well, strain, adorn with fruit and add a little red wine.

SOUTHERN
Juice of 1/2 lemon
Teaspoon of sugar
Glass of Cuban rum
Shake, strain, adorn with fruit and add a little red wine.

STONE
Glass of Plymouth gin
Juice of a lemon
Sweeten with currant syrup.
Shake well, strain into a glass with chipped ice and serve.

TOURAINE
Same as a Whiskey Sour with a dash of Bénédictine and a little red wine.

WHISKEY
Juice of 1/2 lemon
Teaspoon of sugar
Glass of American whiskey
Shake, strain into a medium glass and garnish with fruit.

THE ART OF MAKING A COCKTAIL & MORE

APPLE

Dissolve 1/2 sugar cube with a little water in a large glass.
Chipped ice
Glass of apple jack
Lemon peel
Stir.

BRANDY

Dissolve 1/2 cube of sugar with a little water in a large glass
Chipped ice
Glass of Domecq cognac
Lemon peel
Stir.

GIN

Dissolve 1/2 cube of sugar with a little water in a large glass
Chipped ice
Glass of gin
Lemon peel
Stir.

KENTUCKY

Dissolve 1/2 lump of sugar with a little water in a large glass.
Glass of Bourbon whiskey
Chipped ice
Stir.

MINT

Dissolve 1/3 lump of sugar with a little water in a large glass with 3 sprigs of mint.
Glass of Bourbon whiskey
Chipped ice
Stir.

PEACH
Dissolve 1/12 cube of sugar in a large glass with a little water.
Glass of Peach brandy
Chipped ice
Lemon peel.

PENDENNIS
Dissolve 1/2 sugar cube with a little water in a large glass
Glass of whiskey
Chipped ice.

RUM
Dissolve 1/2 cube of sugar in a large glass with a little water
Glass of Cuban rum
Chipped ice
Lemon peel.

SCOTCH
Dissolve 1/2 lump of sugar in a large glass with a little water
Glass of Scotch whisky
Chipped ice.
Lemon peel.

SOUTHERN

1/2 cube of sugar dissolved in a large glass with a little water
Glass of Bourbon whiskey
Lemon peel and stir.

WHISKEY

Dissolve 1/2 lump of sugar with a little water in a large glass
Glass of Bourbon whiskey
Lemon peel and stir.

BEBIDAS COMPUESTAS
PARA SERVIR EN VASOS DE DISTINTOS TAMAÑOS

AMOR
1/4 Parfait Amour
1/4 yellow Chartreuse
1/4 Bénédictine
Beaten egg white

ARCO IRIS
1/6 Anisette
1/6 crème de cacao
1/6 crème de rosa
1/6 crème de menthe
1/6 crème de Yvette
1/6 Pedro Domecq Fundador Brandy

Be careful not to mix the liquors in the glass, so we can see them separately.

ATENEO
7/8 Dutch maraschino liqueur
1/8 Hungarian apricot brandy

BESO
The yolk of an egg
Teaspoon of sugar
Glass of American whiskey

Shake well and pour mixture into a highball glass half filled with water.

BANDERA
1/3 maraschino liqueur
1/3 grenadine
1/3 crème de Yvette
Pour carefully to avoid mixing, so you can see the 3 colors separately.

BLACK JACK
1/3 iced coffee
1/3 Domecq Tres Cepas
1/3 kirschwasser
Shake well, rub the rim of the glass with lemon peel and sugar.

BRADLEY MARTIN
Crème de menthe shake with 1/5 part of curaçao.

BRANDY FIX (Cognac compuesto)
Squeeze a lemon
1/2 teaspoon of sugar
Glass of pineapple juice
2 dashes of yellow Chartreuse
2/3 glass of Domecq Tres Cepas cognac
Shake, strain into a glass with chipped ice and adorn with fruit.

BRANDY FLOAT (Cognac flotante)
Cover your glass with something larger, invert both tightly so that the cognac is in the smaller glass. Fill seltzer water up to the middle of the larger glass and invert the smaller glass with care so that the cognac floats on the seltzer water.

BRANDY SANGAREE (Sangria de cognac)
Teaspoon of sugar
3/4 Domecq Tres Cepas
1/4 Port wine
Shaved ice in a glass
Shake and strain.

BROCHE
1/2 Domecq cognac
1/2 apricot brandy
Teaspoon of white mint
Dash of absinthe
Shake.

CABALLO BLANCO
A piece of ice
Juice of 1/2 orange
2 dashes of Angostura Bitters
Glass of Scotch whisky
1/2 bottle of ginger ale
Use a large glass.

COLON
The same as a Hot Rye Toddy with Scotch whisky.

CREMA
1/2 teaspoon of Sugar
Glass of milk
Glass of Cuban rum
Shake, strain and add seltzer water.

CRIOLLA
1/4 glass of maraschino liqueur
3/4 glass of Bourbon whiskey
Glass of Madeira wine
2 creezas
Shake and strain into a wine glass.

DE LUXE BRACER
Glass of absinthe
Dashes of French vermouth
Dash of anisette
Dash of yellow Chartreuse
Shake well, strain into a Delmonico glass and add seltzer water.

DOG DAYS (Dias de Perro)
Glass of Scotch whisky
1/2 bottle of ginger ale
2 pieces of orange
A large glass with chipped ice.

DOMINO
2 dashes of Jamaican ginger
Dash of crème de menthe
Glass of raspberry syrup
Glass of Domecq cognac
A little grated nutmeg

DONCELLA
3/4 Bénédictine or crème de cacao
1/4 milk

EDEN
1/2 apricot brandy
1/2 crème de Yvette

ESCOCES
Juice of 1/2 lemon
Glass of Scotch whisky
Pieces of ice
A little sugar
Fill the glass with seltzer water.

FAUSTO
1/2 lemon
2 dashes of Amer Picon
Glass of English gin
Pieces of ice in a tall glass
Fill with seltzer

FLOATER (Flotador)
3/4 Russian kümmel
1/4 Domecq cognac

GINEBRA COMPUESTA
Glass with ice cubes
Teaspoon or sugar
3 dashes of Angostura Bitters
Mint
Glass of Dutch gin

GOLDEN DREAM (Sueño Dorado)
Juice of 1/2 lemon
Teaspoon of sugar
Yolk of an egg
Glass of English gin
Shake, strain and add seltzer water.

GOLDEN SLIPPER (Zapatilla de Oro)
1/2 yellow Chartreuse
An egg
Fill the glass with Eau de Vie de Dantzig

GREEN TIE (Corbata verde)
1/2 green crème de menthe
1/2 crème de rosa

GUACHINANGO
Use a tall, fine glass
Glass of English gin
Squeeze a lemon
Bottle of clear Polar beer
Ice cubes

GUAJIRO

In a medium glass, put a teaspoon of honey or sugar syrup and add the amount of Cuban rum you desire.

HARVESTER (LABRADOR)

Glass of orange juice
1/2 glass of English gin
Shake with chipped ice and strain into a wine glass.

IRISH ROSE (ROSA IRLANDESA)

A highball of Irish whiskey with 3 or 4 dashes of grenadine.

JERSEY LILY POUSSE CAFE

1/2 green Chartreuse
1/2 Domecq cognac
10 dashes of Angostura bitters
Pour the cognac with care so that they don't mix and serve.

JERSEY SUNSET (PUESTA DE SOL EN JERSEY)

1/2 glass of syrup
Glass of natural water
Lemon peel
Chipped ice in a glass
Add 2 dashes of Angostura Bitters carefully on the mixture.

JUNE ROSE (Rosa de Junio)
Juice of 1/2 lemon
Juice of an orange
1/2 glass of English gin
1/2 glass raspberry liqueur
Shake, strain and fill glass with seltzer.

KING'S CORDIAL (Cordial del Rey)
3/4 maraschino liqueur
1/4 Scotch whisky

KNICKERBEIN
1/2 glass of Bénédictine
Yolk of an egg
3 dashes of kümmel
Dash of Angostura Bitters
Use a regular size glass and take care not to mix the various ingredients.

KNICKERBOCKER
1/4 glass of raspberry syrup
Juice of a lemon
Glass of Cuban rum
2 dashes of dark curaçao
Shake, strain into a glass with chipped ice and garnish with fruit.

MACAGUA
White of an egg
Glass of Domecq cognac
1/2 teaspoon of sugar
Shake and strain into a wine glass.

MAMIE TAYLOR
Large pieces of ice
Glass of Scotch whisky
Juice of 1/2 lemon
Bottle of ginger ale
Stir well.

MAMIE TAYLOR SOUTHERN STYLE
Use a tall glass
Lemon peel strip hung on the glass
Glass of Scotch whisky
Ice cubes
Bottle of ginger ale

MARTINIQUE (Martinica)
1/3 Bénédictine
1/3 kümmel
1/3 milk

MOJO CRIOLLO
Glass of Cuban rum
Dashes of lemon
Teaspoon of sugar
Serve in a medium glass with ice and a spoon.

MONTECARLO
Juice of 1/2 lemon
1/2 teaspoon of sugar
Glass of Gordon's gin
White of an egg
2 dashes of assorted liquors

MORNING BRACER
1/3 white absinthe
2/3 Italian vermouth
Shake well, strain into a Delmonico glass and fill with seltzer water.

MORNING STAR (ESTRELLA MATINAL)
Glass of milk
1/2 glass or Port wine
1/4 Scotch whisky
An egg
Shake, strain into a tall glass and fill with seltzer.

OJEN (ESTILO NEW ORLEANS)
Glass of Ojen
2 dashes Peychaud bitters
Shake well with crushed ice and and serve in a glass of white wine.

OSO POLAR
1/2 bottle of cider
1/2 bottle of dark Polar beer

WHITE CAP (GORRA BLANCA)
Bénédictine over milk.

PALACIO CRISTAL
2 dashes of orange bitters
3/4 English gin
1/4 crème de Yvette
Shake.

PARISIAN (Parisién)
Glass of Byrrh wine
Juice of a lemon
Chipped ice in a glass
Stir, fill with seltzer water and serve.

PARISIAN POUSSE CAFE
(Pousse café Parisién)
2/5 dark curaçao
2/5 kirschwasser
1/5 Chartreuse
Use a pousse café glass.

PEACH BLOW
Juice of 1/2 lemon
Teaspoon of sugar
Glass of English gin
Half of a peach
Shake, strain and fill glass with seltzer.

PELUCHE
1/2 American whiskey
14 maraschino liqueur
An egg
Small bottle of milk
Shake, strain into a fine glass and serve.

PERFECTO
Use a large glass
4 pieces of ice
Dash of lemon juice
Lump of sugar
2 slices of pineapple
Fill glass with Champagne
Dash of Angostura Bitters
Decorate with fruit.

PORTER SHANDY
Half a glass of dark Polar beer
Half a glass of Light Polar beer

PORT STARBOARD
1/2 Curaçao
1/2 yellow Chartreuse
Use a pousse café glass.

POUSSE CAFE NO. 1
1/6 raspberry syrup
1/6 maraschino liqueur
1/6 crème de menthe (green)
1/6 dark curaçao
1/6 yellow Chartreuse
1/6 Pedro Domecq Fundador Brandy
Use a pousse café glass and pour carefully to avoid mixing the colors.

POUSSE CAFE NO. 2

1/5 Grenadine syrup
1/5 anisette
1/5 crème de Yvette
1/5 Chartreuse (green)
1/5 Pedro Domecq Fundador Brandy

Use a pousse café glass and pour carefully to avoid mixing the colors.

POUSSE L'AMOUR

1/3 maraschino liqueur
Yolk of an egg
1/3 Bénédictine
1/3 Pedro Domecq Fundador Brandy
Glass of regular size.

PROMOTER

Juice of 1/2 lemon
Teaspoon of sugar
Glass of sloe gin
Chipped ice
An egg

Shake well, strain and fill glass with seltzer water.

QUEEN CHARLOTTE (Reina Carlota)

1/4 glass raspberry syrup
Glass of French red wine
Pieces of ice
Bottle of lemon soda
Stir well.

RENAUD'S POUSSE CAFE
1/3 maraschino liqueur
1/3 curaçao
1/3 Pedro Domecq Fundador Brandy
Use a medium glass.

SAM WARD
Put chipped ice into a cocktail glass, a lemon peel all around the interior of the glass and fill with yellow Chartreuse or other liqueur you want.

SHANDY GAFF
Medium glass of light Polar beer
Medium glass of ginger ale or soda.

SHERRY AND BITTERS
(Jerez y Amargo de Angostura)
Dashes of Angostura bitters and fill glass with Jerez La Ina.

SILVER DREAM
(Sueño de Plata)
Juice of 1/2 lemon
1/2 teaspoon of sugar
White of an egg
Glass of English gin
Shake well, strain into a wine glass, add a little seltzer water and serve.

SINGLE STANDARD
Bourbon whiskey rickey in a glass of lemonade.

SNOWBALL (BOLA DE NIEVE)
White of an egg
Teaspoon of sugar
Glass of Cuban rum
Shake, strain and fill glass with ginger ale.

SODA NEGUS PUNCH BOWL
4 dashes of Angostura bitters
1/2 bottle of Port wine
10 to 12 sugar cubes
12 cloves of spice
Teaspoon of grated nutmeg
Put these ingredients in a saucepan, heat and stir well, but do not boil. Allow the mixture to cool and add a bottle of soda.

SOOTHER (SEDOSO)
Juice of 1/2 lemon
Teaspoon of sugar
1/4 Domecq Tres Cepas
1/4 aguardiente de manazana
1/4 curaçao
Shake, strain and serve in a glass with crushed ice.

EL ARTE DE HACER UN COCKTAIL Y ALGO MAS

SOUL KISS (Beso del alma)
1/2 teaspoon of sugar
Juice of an orange
1/2 Byrrh wine
1/4 American whiskey
1/4 French vermouth
Shake, strain into a large glass and will with seltzer.

SPECIAL
Glass of orange juice
Glass of lemon juice
Glass of English gin
Teaspoon of sugar
Shake well, add crushed ice and serve in a glass.

ST. CROIX RUM CRUSTA
3/dashes of syrup
Dash of Angostura bitters
Dash of orange bitters
Glass of St Croix rum
2 or 3 dashes of maraschino liqueur
Mix well and strain into a large glass. Put a lemon peel on the rim and add a little sugar and seltzer water.

STINGER (Punzante)
1/2 Pedro Domecq Fundador Brandy cognac
1/2 white crème de menthe
Lemon peel
Shake and strain into a cocktail glass.

STONEWALL (PARED DE CANTERIA)
Teaspoon of sugar
2 pieces of ice
Glass of American whiskey
Bottle of soda.
Stir well with a spoon and serve.

SUKA
1/2 maraschino liqueur
1/2 crème de Yvette
A cherry

SUISSESS
3/4 white absinthe
1/4 anisette
White of an egg
Shake well and serve in a Delmonico glass.

SUISETTE
Juice of 1/2 lemon
2 dashes of absinthe
Teaspoon of sugar
1/2 Italian vermouth
2/3 Domecq Tres Cepas brandy
Shake, strain into a large glass and fill with seltzer water.

SUSIE TAYLOR
Juice of 1/2 lemon
Glass of Cuban rum
1/2 bottle of ginger ale

TEA SHAKE (The batido)
Glass of tea
An egg
1/2 teaspoon of sugar
Shake well and strain into a wine glass.

THREE QUARTER (tres cuartos)
1/3 yellow Chartreuse
1/3 curaçao
1/3 Pedro Domecq Fundador Brandy

TIT FLOAT
Curaçao with a little milk shaken. Put a bit of cherry in the center and serve.

TIP TOP BRACER
Put ice in a highball glass
1/4 carbonated mineral water
2 dashes of Celery bitters (amargo de apio)
A little salt
Stir and serve.

TOBBIE TOBIAS
1/2 Domecq Tres Cepas cognac
1/2 Apricot brandy
Lemon peel
Shake and strain into a cocktail glass.

TWENTIEH CENTURY (Siglo XX)
Juice of 1/2 lemon
Teaspoon of sugar
Glass of Bourbon whiskey
Dashes of Cuban rum
Shake well, strain into a highball glass and complete with seltzer water or ginger ale.

VIUDA
1/2 glass of orange juice
Glass of American whiskey
2 Dashes of Cuban rum
Squeeze a lemon peel.

VIUDA ALEGRE
2/3 Bénédictine
An egg
Glass of milk
Shake, strain and serve.

VERMOUTH ACHAMPANADO
Fill a medium glass with ice, put a teaspoon of sugar, fill halfway with Italian vermouth and the rest with soda.

VERMOUTH A LA AMERICANA
Glass of Italian vermouth
2 dashes of Angostura bitters
1/2 teaspoon of sugar
Decorate with a morello cherry.

WHISKEY FIX (WHISKEY COMPUESTO)
Teaspoon of sugar
Juice of 1/2 lemon
Glass of Scotch whisky
Shake, strain in to a glass decorated with fruit.

WHISKEY FLOAT
Into a half glass of carbonated water, slowly pour a glass of American whiskey and serve.

YANKEE
Glass of American whiskey
2 cubes of ice
Fill glass with cider, stir well and serve.

DRINKS INDEX

–A–

ABSINTHE (Ajenjo) ... 141
ABSINTHE DRIP ... 141
ABSINTHE ... 21
ADALOR ... 153
ADAN ... 21
ADONIS ... 21
ALASKA ... 21
ALCALDE (MAYOR) ... 21
ALEXANDER ... 22
ALFONSO XIII ... 22
ALMASQUE ... 22
ALMENDARES ... 22
ALONSO NANO ... 23
ALVARADO ... 23
AMER PICON POUFFLE ... 123
AMER PICON POUFFLE ... 187
AMER PICON ... 145
AMER PICON ... 215
AMERICAN BEAUTY (belleza americana) ... 153
AMERICAN CLUB ... 23
AMERICAN GROG ... 181
AMOR ... 229
ANGEL DREAM ... 23
ANGEL KISS ... 23
ANGEL ... 23
ANGOSTURA GINGER ALE ... 187
ANGOSTURA PHOSPHATE ... 187
ANGOSTURA SODA ... 187
ANGOSTURA ... 123
ANTILLAS ... 24
APPLE ... 223
APPLEJACK ... 24
APRICOT ... 24
ARCO IRIS ... 229
ARCTIC (Artico) ... 153
ARDSLEY ... 187
ARDSLEY ... 24

ARMENTEROS 24
ARMOUR... 25
ASSORTED SHAKES (FRAPES SURTIDOS) 141
ASTOR PUNCH (ponche Astor) 153
ASTORIA.. 25
ATENEO 229
AUTOCLUB 25
AUTOMOBILE.. 188
AVIACION.. 25

—B—

BACARDI 25
BALLANTINE 26
BALTIMORE BRACER 13
BAMBOO.. 26
BANDERA 230
BARACCAS 26
BARRY.. 26
BAYARD... 123
BEADLESTONE 26
BEATA 27
BEAUTY (Linda) 27
BEAUTY SPOT (Lunar) 27
BEER SHANDY 188
BERMUDA.. 145
BESO 229
BIJOU 27
BILL MEYER PUCH.. 154
BILLY TAYLOR... 188
BILTMORE... 27
BIRD (Pajaro) 28
BIRD OF PARADISE (ave del Paraiso) 123
BISHOP (Obispo) 28
BISHOP POTTER.. 28
BISHOP PUNCH (Jarra)... 154
BISMARCK... 124
BLACK & WHITE (Blanco y Negro) 29
BLACK HAWK (HALCON NEGRO) 28
BLACK HORN 28

BLACK JACK 230
BLACKSTONE (Piedra Negra) 29
BLACKSTONE EXTRA 29
BLACKSTONE NECTAR 154
BLACKSTONE 188
BLANCO-HERRERA J. 29
BLANQUITA R. 29
BLUE BLAZER (llamarada azul) 181
BLUE MOUNT (Monte azul) 30
BOBBIE BURNS (for two) 30
BOLES 30
BOOBY 30
BORDELAISE PUNCH (Ponche bordalesa) 155
BOSTON MILK PUNCH (Ponche de leche Boston) 155
BOSTON 188
BOURBON COLLINS 101
BOURBON WHISKEY PUNCH / RYE WHISKEY PUNCH 156
BOURBON 145
BOWMAN 30
BRADLEY MARTIN 230
BRAIN DUSTER 13
BRANDY (De cognac) 115
BRANDY (Cognac) 149
BRANDY (Cognac) 31
BRANDY (de Cognac) 124
BRANDY (de Cognac) 135
BRANDY (de Cognac) 145
BRANDY CAMPRELLE 13
BRANDY COLLINS 101
BRANDY CRUSTA 13
BRANDY FIX (Cognac compuesto) 230
BRANDY FLOAT (Cognac flotante) 231
BRANDY PUNCH (Ponche de cognac) 155
BRANDY SANGAREE (Sangria de cognac) 231
BRANDY SCAFFA 13
BRANDY 207
BRANDY 211
BRANDY 215
BRANDY 223
BRANDY-MILK PUNCH (Ponche de cognac y leche) 154

BRANT 31
BRIDAL (Nupcial) 31
BRIGHTON 31
BROCHE 231
BRONX DRY (Seco) 32
BRONX TERRACE 32
BRONX 32
BROOKLYN 31
BROWN (Carmelita) 32
BRUNSWICK PUNCH 156
BRUNSWICK 215
BRUT (Estilo frances) 32
BULL MOOSE PUNCH 157
BULL POLAR 189
BULL 189
BULLS EYE (Ojo de toro) 156
BURGUNDY (Borgona) 156
BUSH (Manigua) 33
BUSSE 135
BYRRH 33

—C—

C. A. C. (Club Atletico) 35
CABALLO BLANCO 231
CABINET 33
CAFE AU KIRSCH 33
CAFE BOULES 181
CAFE DE PARIS 33
CALISAYA 34
CAMAGUEYANO 34
CAMPUZANO PACKARD 34
CANADIAN (Canadiense) 124
CANADIAN WHISKEY 215
CANADIAN WHISKEY (de whiskey canadiense) 124
CANDADO (Jabon) 34
CARDINAL PUNCH 157
CARIBE 181
CASINO 34
CAT (Gato) 35

CERVECERO 35
CHAMPAGNE ADONIS 157
CHAMPAGNE COBBLER 17
CHAMPAGNE EXTRA 158
CHAMPAGNE POLAR (A one gallon punch bowl) 158
CHAMPAGNE PUNCH No. 2 159
CHAMPAGNE PUNCH (Ponche de Champagne) 159
CHAMPAGNE 216
CHAMPAGNE 35
CHAMPOLA DE ANON 189
CHAMPOLA DE GUANABANA 189
CHANTECLER 35
CHARLIE CHAPLIN 36
CHERRY BLOSSOM (Flor de Cerezo) 36
CHICAGO 125
CHINA 36
CHIQUITICA 190
CHIQUITICA 36
CHOCOLATE AMBROSIA 36
CHOCOLATE CREAM SODA 190
CHOCOLATE 115
CHOCOLATE 135
CINCINNATI 37
CLARA 37
CLARET (de vino tinto) 125
CLARET PUNCH No. 1 159
CLARET PUNCH No. 2 160
CLARET PUNCH No. 3 160
CLIFTON LILY 37
CLOVER CLUB 37
CLOVER LEAF 37
CLUB DE CANTINEROS 38
COBBLER DE POLAR 18
COBBLER DE VINO DE JEREZ 17
COBBLER DE VINO PORTO 17
COBBLER DE VINO TINTO 18
COBBLER DE WHISKEY 18
COBBLER DEVINO DEL RHIN 18
COBBLER ESPANOL 17
COFFEE (Cafe) 38

COFFEE (de Cafe) ... 135
COGNAC (Brandy) ... 119
COGNAC QUEMADO CON MELOCOTON ... 182
COLLEGE WIDOW ... 38
COLON ... 182
COLON ... 232
COLON ... 38
COLONIAL O MILLER (para dos) ... 38
COMANDANTE DR. FIGUERAS ... 39
COMBINATION PUNCH ... 160
CONCHITA A. ... 39
CONCLAVE ... 161
CONEY ... 39
CONGRESO ... 39
CONSOLIDATED (Consolidado) ... 39
CORNELL ... 40
CORONATION (Coronacion) ... 40
COUNTRY CLUB ... 190
COUNTRY CLUB ... 40
CREAM (de Leche) ... 136
CREAM PUNCH (Ponche crema) ... 161
CREMA ... 232
CREOLE (Criollo) ... 40
CREOLE PUNCH (Ponche criolla) ... 161
CRESCENT ... 40
CRIOLLA ... 232
CRIOLLO ... 182
CRUSELLAS R. F. ... 41
CUBAN MILK PUNCH (Ponche de leche a la Cubana) ... 161
CUBANO ... 41
CURAÇAO PUNCH ... 162
CUSHMAN ... 41

—D—

DAIQUIRI DULCE ... 41
DAIQUIRI ... 41
DAISY ... 125
DE LUXE BRACER ... 232
DELMONICO ... 42

DIAMOND (Diamante) 125
DIMAS 42
DIXIE 42
DOG DAYS (Dias de Perro) 232
DOMINO 233
DON EMETERIO 42
DONCELLA 233
DORADO 42
DOUBLE STANDARD 216
DOUGLAS FAIRBANKS 43
DOWN (Abajo) 43
DREAM (Sueno) 43
DRY GIN FIZZ 125
DUBONNET 43
DUCHESS (Duquesa) 43
DUKE (Duque) 44
DUNHAM 190
DUPLEX 44
DURKEE 190
DUTCH CHARLIE'S 44

—E—

ECHARTE, J.L. 44
EDEN 233
EGG (de Huevo) 136
EGG PHOSPHATE 191
EGG 216
ELMWOOD PUNCH 162
EMERALD (Esmeralda) 44
EMERSON 44
EMPRESS PUNCH (Ponche Emperatariz) 162
ENSALADA 191
ESCOCES 233
EVA 45
EWING 45
EXPRESO 45

—F—

FANCY (Cognac, Gin or Whiskey) 45
FARMER'S (Campesino) 45
FASCISTA 46
FAUSTO 233
FAVORITA 46
FISH HOUSE PUNCH (en conserva) 163
FISH HOUSE PUNCH (Ponche pescaderia) 162
FLOATER (Flotador) 233
FLORODORA (Estil Imperial) 191
FLORODORA 191
FLUSHING 46
FOUR DOLLAR (Cuatro pesos) 46
FOURTH DEGREE (Cuatro grado) 46
FOURTH REGIMENT (4.0 Regimiento) 47
FOX SHOT (Tiro de Zorra) 47
FRANCO (Aviador espanol) 47
FRANK HILL 47
FRENCH CANADIAN 47

—G—

GALVEZ 126
GAMBRINUS 191
GAMBRINUS 48
GARCIA MIER 163
GIBSON 48
GIN (De ginebra) 115
GIN (de Ginebra) 126
GIN (de Ginebra) 136
GIN (de ginebra) 203
GIN (Ginebra) 149
GIN (GINEBRA) 145
GIN BUCK 203
GIN PUNCH (Ponche de ginebra) 163
GIN 207
GIN 211
GIN 216
GIN 223

GIN	48
GINEBRA COMPUESTA	234
GINGER (de Jenjibre)	115
GINGER ALE (sin licores)	164
GINGER ALE	164
GINGER ALE	192
GLORIA SWANSON	126
GOLDEN (de Oro)	126
GOLDEN DREAM (Sueño Dorado)	234
GOLDEN SLIPPER (Zapatilla de Oro)	234
GOLF	48
GOOD FELLOW (Buen chico)	48
GOOD TIMES (Rumba)	49
GOODMAN PUNCH	164
GRAHAM	49
GRAND DUKE	127
GRAPE JUICE (Zumo de Uva)	165
GRAPE JUICE (de zumo de Uva)	149
GRAPE JUICE (sin licores)	165
GRAPE JUICE (Zumo de uva)	192
GREEN TIE (Corbata verde)	234
GRENADINE (Granadina)	127
GRENADINE	217
GRENADINE-GIN	217
GRIT	49
GUACHINANGO	234
GUAJIRO	235
GUGGENHEIM	49

—H—

HABANA	192
HABANA	49
HANCOCK	217
HARDING PUNCH	165
HARRIET (Enriqueta)	50
HART	50
HARVARD	50
HARVESTER (Labrador)	235
HARVESTER	50

HAWAII 192
HEARST 50
HERALD PUNCH 166
HIGHLAND (Montana) 115
HIGHSTEPPER 51
HILLARD 51
HIPOLITO REGUERO 51
HOLLAND (Holanda) 127
HOLSTEIN 51
HOMESTEAD (Hogar) 51
HONOLULU 52
HOT AMERICAN GROG 182
HOT APPLEJACK TODDY 183
HOT CLARET PUNCH (ponche caliente de vino tinto) 183
HOT LEMONADE (limonada caliente) 183
HOT MILK PUNCH 183
HOT SPICED RUM 184
HOWARD 51
HUDSON 52
HUNGARIAN BRACER 14
HUNTER (Cazador) 52

—I—

ICE CREAM SODA 192
IDEAL 52
IMPERIO 53
INFURIATOR 52
IRIS 53
IRISH (Irlandes) 127
IRISH COLLINS 101
IRISH ROSE (Rosa Irlandesa) 146
IRISH ROSE (rosa irlandesa) 235
IRISH WHISKEY (Whiskey Escocés) 193
IRISH WHISKEY PUNCH (ponche de whiskey irlandes) 166
IRISH WHISKEY 217
IRISH 207
IRVING 53
ISABELLE 53
ITALIANO 53

—J—

JACK ROSE 54
JACK ZELLER 54
JAP (Japones) 128
JAPANESE 54
JENKS 54
JEREZ (Sherry) 119
JEREZ CON HUEVO 119
JERSEY LILY POUSSE CAFE 235
JERSEY LILY 54
JERSEY SUNSET (Puesta de sol en Jersey) 235
JERSEY 217
JERSEY 54
JIM LEE 55
JIMMIE LANIER 55
JOCKEY CLUB 55
JOHN COLLINS 102
JOSE MIGUEL 55
JUDGE (Juez) 55
JUNE (Junio) 116
JUNE ROSE (Rosa de Junio) 236
JUVENTUD ASTURIANA 56

—K—

K D T 193
KENTUCKY COLONEL 56
KENTUCKY MINT (de yerbabuena a lo Kentuckiano) .. 149
KENTUCKY 223
KHATURA 193
KIKI 193
KING COLE 128
KING'S CORDIAL (Cordial del Rey) 236
KISS WALTZ (Vals del Beso) 56
KNICKERBEIN 236
KNICKERBOCKER PUNCH 166
KNICKERBOCKER 236

—L—

LADIES (señoras)	56
LALLA HOOK	128
LAVIN	57
LEMON PHOSPHATE	193
LEMONADES	194
LEONORA	57
LEWIS	57
LIBERAL	57
LILLO	57
LIMONADA ANGOSTURA	194
LIMONADA APOLLINARIS	194
LIMONADA CLUB SODA	194
LIMONADA CON AGUA DE SELTZ	195
LIMONADA CON GASEOSA	195
LIMONADA CON WHISKEY	196
LIMONADA DE VINO TINTO	194
LIMONADA EGG (de huevo)	194
LIMONADA FRUIT (de frutas)	195
LIMONADA NARANJADA	195
LOFTUS	58
LOMA TENNIS	58
LONDON (Londres)	58
LONE TREE (Arbol solitario)	58
LORD BALTIMORE	166
LORD LATOUNNE	167
LOVE (Amor)	58
LUCAS PEREZ	59
LUSITANIA	59

—M—

MACAGUA	236
MAMIE TAYLOR SOUTHERN STYLE	237
MAMIE TAYLOR	237
MANCHURIA	59
MANHATTAN	59
MANOLO SANTEIRO	60
MARCONI	60

MARGOT	60
MARIA M.	60
MARIANAO	61
MARIETA	60
MARTINI (Extra)	61
MARTINI DRY (Seco)	61
MARTINI	61
MARTINIQUE (Martinica)	237
MARY GARDEN	61
MARY PICKFORD	62
MAUSER	62
MAZAGRAN	196
Mc LANE	63
McDONALD	62
McHENRY	62
MERRY WIDOW (Viuda Alegre)	128
MERRY WIDOW (Viuda Alegre)	63
MERRY WIDOW	167
METROPOLITAN (al estilo del Sur)	63
METROPOLITAN	63
MEXICO	129
MIAMI	63
MILK (de leche)	167
MILK SHAKE	168
MILLER	64
MILLIONAIRE (millonario)	167
MILLIONAIRE (Millonario)	64
MILLIONAIRE	218
MILO	64
MINT (yerbabuena)	168
MINT (Yerbabuena)	196
MINT WESTERN STYLE (de yerbabuena a lo Occidental)	150
MINT	211
MINT	223
MIRAMAR YACHT CLUB	64
MOJO CRIOLLO	237
MONCAYO	64
MONTANA	65
MONTECARLO	237
MONTICELLO	168

MORA 196
MORNING (Manana) 65
MORNING BRACER 238
MORNING GLORY 129
MORNING STAR (estrella matinal) 238
MOSELLE WINE (Vino Mosela) 168
MULL CLARET 184

—N—

NANA 65
NARANJA MAMBI 197
NARRAGANSETT 196
NARRAGANSETT 65
NECTAR POLAR 169
NENA A. 65
NENA R. 66
NEW ORLEANS (Nueva Orleans) 129
NEW YORK 66
NICHOLAS 66
NOBLE 66
NOEL 66
NORTH POLE (Polo Norte) 67
NUTTING 67

—O—

OJEN (estilo New Orleans) 238
OJEN (Cocktail de Ojen a la espanola) 67
OLD FASHION (Estilo antiguo) 67
OLIVETTE 68
OPALO 68
OPERA 68
ORANGE BLOSSOM (Azahar) 68
OSO POLAR 238
OSO POLAR 69
OYSTER BAY 69

—P—

PALACIO CRISTAL	238
PALL MALL	146
PALM BEACH	69
PALMA REAL	69
PALMETTO	69
PAN-AMERICANO	70
PARADISE (Paraiso)	70
PARISIAN (Parisién)	239
PARISIAN POUSSE CAFE	239
PARISIAN	70
PARSON	70
PEACH BLOW	239
PEACH BRANDY (de aguariente de melocoton)	169
PEACH	224
PEACOCK (Pavo Real)	71
PEBLO	70
PELUCHE	239
PENDENNIS	224
PEPIN RIVERO	71
PERFECTO	240
PERLA JAPONESA	71
PERLA DE ORIENTE	71
PHEASANT (Faisan)	71
PHILADELPHIA SPECIAL	72
PICK ME UP (Levantame)	72
PICON	72
PIÑA BLOSSOM	73
PIÑA BRONX	73
PIÑA	169
PINE TREE (pino)	72
PING-PONG	72
PLAYA MARIANAO	73
PLAZA HOTEL	73
PLUS ULTRA ESPANOL	73
POEMA	74
POLAR	169
POLAR	197
POLAR	74

POLLY 129
POLO FARM 74
POLO 74
POMPIER (Bombero) 146
PONY 170
PORT STARBOARD 240
PORT WINE (de vino Oporto) 136
PORT WINE NEGUS 184
PORT WINE SANGAREE (sangria of Port wine) 197
PORTER OR PAT'S 74
PORTER SHANDY 240
PORTO RICO (Puerto Rico) 203
POUSSE CAFE NO. 1 240
POUSSE CAFE NO. 2 241
POUSSE L'AMOUR 241
PRAIRIE (Pradera) 75
PRESIDENTE MACHADO 75
PRESIDENTE 75
PRIMO DE RIVERA 75
PRINCESS LILLIAN 75
PRINCETON 76
PRINCIPE DE ASTURIAS (Prince of Asturias) 76
PRINCIPE DE GALES (Prince of Wales) 76
PROMOTER 241
PUENTES 76

—Q—

QUEEN (Reina) 77
QUEEN CHARLOTTE (Reina Carlota) 241

—R—

REGENT 170
REIS 77
REMSEN 197
REMUS 130
RENAUD'S POUSSE CAFE 242
REVIVER (Resucitador) 136
RHINE WINE (vino del Rhin) 171

RHINE WINE (de vino del Rhin) 170
RHINE WINE AND SELTZER 198
RIDING CLUB (Club de Equitacion) 77
ROB ROY 77
ROBERT BURNS 77
ROBERT E. LEE 198
ROMAN (a la Romana) 171
ROMANO 78
RON 116
RON 119
ROOSEVELT 172
ROOSEVELT 218
ROSA 78
ROSSINGTON 78
ROYAL GIN (Ginebra Real) 130
ROYAL SMILE (Sonrisa Real) 78
RUBIN 78
RUBY ROYAL 79
RUBY 79
RUM (de ron) 172
RUM COLLINS 102
RUM 207
RUM 218
RUM 224
RYE (de whiskey de centeno) 146
RYE COLLINS 102

—S—

SABBATH (Sabatino) 198
SABBATH (Sabatino) 79
SABROSOS 172
SALOME 173
SALOME 79
SAM WARD 242
SANGAREE POLAR (Sangria de Cerveza Polar) 198
SANGAREE SHERRY (Sangria de vino Jerez) 198
SANSON 80
SARATOGA 218
SARATOGA 80

SARDINERO 80
SAUTERNES (al estilo del Sur) 174
SAUTERNES CUP 173
SAUTERNES 173
SAXON 80
SCHEUER 80
SCHLEY 174
SCOTCH (de whiskey Escoces) 146
SCOTCH (Escocés) 199
SCOTCH COLLINS 103
SCOTCH WHISKY (de whiskey Escoces) 130
SCOTCH WHISKY (de whiskey Escoces) 174
SCOTCH 207
SCOTCH 219
SCOTCH 224
SEA SIDE (Orilla del mar) 199
SEÑORITA 81
SEPTEMBER MORNING (Manana de Stbre.) 81
SERGIO CARBO 81
SHANDY GAFF 242
SHERIDAN 175
SHERMAN 81
SHERRY (de vino de Jerez) 137
SHERRY (Jerez) 81
SHERRY AND BITTERS (Jerez y Amargo de Angostura) 242
SIDRA CUP (Cider) 175
SIDRA CUP (sin licores) 175
SIDRA POLAR 176
SILVER (Plata) 130
SILVER (Plata) 82
SILVER BOWL 131
SILVER DREAM (sueño de plata) 242
SILVER 219
SINGLE STANDARD 243
SLOE GIN FIZZ 131
SLOME 82
SLOPPY JOE 82
SMITH 82
SNOW BOWL 131
SNOWBALL (Bola de nieve) 243

SOCIETY (Sociedad) 82
SODA NEGUS PUNCH BOWL 243
SODA 83
SOOTHER (Sedoso) 243
SOOTHER 176
SOUL KISS (Beso del alma) 244
SOUL KISS (Beso del alma) 83
SOUTH AFRICA (Africa del Sur) 83
SOUTHERN 219
SOUTHERN 225
SOUVENIR 83
SPAULDING 83
SPECIAL 176
SPECIAL 244
SPHINX (Esfinge) 84
ST. CROIX RUM CRUSTA 244
ST. FRANCIS (San Francisco) 84
ST. JOHN (San Juan) 84
ST. PETER (San Pedro) 84
STAR (a la antigua) 85
STAR (Estrella) 116
STAR (Estrella) 84
STEINHART 85
STEINWAY 177
STINGER (Punzante) 244
STONE 219
STONEWALL (pared de canteria) 245
STORY (Cuento) 85
STRAWBERRY (de Fresa) 131
SUISETTE 245
SUISSESS 245
SUKA 245
SUNSET (Puesta de Sol) 86
SUNSHINE (Luz Solar) for two 85
SUNSHINE (Luz Solar) 131
SUSIE TAYLOR 245
SWAN (Cisne) 86

—T—

TANGO	86
TAXI	86
TEA SHAKE (The batido)	246
THREE QUARTER (tres cuartos)	246
TIP TOP BRACER	246
TIP TOP	87
TIQUI	86
TIT FLOAT	246
TITINA	87
TOBBIE TOBIAS	246
TOM AND JERRY	184
TOM COLLINS	103
TOM GIN FIZZ	132
TORONJA BRONX	87
TOURAINE	220
TREASURY (Tesoreria)	87
TRILBY	88
TRINIDAD	88
TROWBRIDGE	88
TRUFFIN	88
TU Y YO	89
TULANE	88
TURF AMERICANO	89
TURF ARGENTINO	89
TURK'S NECK	177
TUXEDO	89
TWENTIEH CENTURY (Siglo XX)	247
TWO SPOT (Dos maracas)	90

—U—

ULLOA	90
UNION CLUB (Habana)	90
UNION CLUB	90
UZCUDUM	199
UZCUDUM	90

—V—

VALENTINO	91
VAN WYCK	91
VEDADO TENNIS	91
VELVET	177
VERMOUTH ACHAMPANADO	91
VERMOUTH A LA AMERICANA	247
VERMOUTH ACHAMPANADO	247
VERMOUTH LA AMERICANA	91
VERMOUTH	120
VERRACO	92
VETERANO	92
VIENNA	92
VIOLET (Violeta)	132
VIRGEN LOCA	92
VIUDA ALEGRE	247
VIUDA	247
VOLUNTARIO	93

—W—

WALDORF EXTRA	178
WALDORF QUEEN'S	93
WALDORF SPECIAL	93
WALDORF	132
WALDORF	177
WALDORF	93
WARD LINE	94
WAXEN	94
WEST INDIA (Antilla)	94
WHILE AWAY (Ausente)	94
WHISKEY (a la antigua)	178
WHISKEY FIX (whiskey compuesto)	248
WHISKEY FLOAT	248
WHISKEY	116
WHISKEY	120
WHISKEY	132
WHISKEY	207
WHISKEY	211

WHISKEY	220
WHISKEY	225
WHISKEY	94
WHISKEY-GRANADINA	132
WHITE (Blanco)	199
WHITE CAP (gorra blanca)	238
WHITE ELEPHANT (Elefante blanco)	95
WHITE RAT (Rata blanca)	95
WHITE ROSE (Rosa blanca)	95
WILLIAM GODRON	95
WILSON	95
WONDER (Milagro)	96

—XY—

YACHT CLUB	96
YALE	96
YANKEE PRINCESS (Princesa Yankee)	97
YANKEE	248
YANKEE	96
YORK	97

—Z—

ZABRISKIE	97
ZARZAPARRILLA	199
ZAZA	98
ZAZARAC	97
ZORRICHIQUI	98
ZORRILLA	98

Also published by Mixellany Limited:

Bariana [French edition]
Café Royal Cocktail Book by William Tarling
Champagne Cocktails, Revised and expanded 2010 edition
Cuba: The Legend of Rum
gaz regan's Annual Manual for Bartenders, 2011
Mixellany's Annotated Bariana
Mixellany's Bariana: The Collector's Edition
Mixologist: The Journal of the American Cocktail, Volume 1
Mixologist: The Journal of the American Cocktail, Volume 2
Mixologist: The Journal of the European Cocktail, Volume 3
Pioneers of Mixing at Elite Bars: 1903-1933
Spirituous Journey: A History of Dirnk, Book Two
Spirituous Journey: A History of Drink, Book One
The Book of Bourbon and Other fine American Whiskies
The Cocktailian Chronicles: Life with the Professor, Volume 1
The Mixellany Guide to Gin
The Soul of Brasil

Available at www.mixellany.com

www.ingramcontent.com/pod-product-compliance
Lightning Source LLC
LaVergne TN
LVHW041331080426
835512LV00006B/402